PLAN of the SPILSBY CIRCUIT, &c.

...preach the Gospel. ROM. x. 15.

29	FEBRUARY 5	12	19	26	MARCH 5	12	19	26	APRIL 2	9	16	23	30	MAY 7	14	21	28		PREACHERS.
1	··	2	··	1	··	2	··	1	··	2	··	1	··	2	··	1	··	1	Howarth
··	1	··	2	··	1	··	2	··	1	··	2	··	1	··	2	··	1	2	Keeling
2	··	1	··	2	··	1	··	2	··	1	··	2	··	1	··	2	··	3	Brackenbury, Esq.
··	6	··	12	··	9	··	10	··	13	··	3	··	4	··	3	··	13	4	Joll
··	4	··	10	··	16	··	13	··	7	··	11	··	9	··	10	··	12	5	Hoyles
··	12	··	13	··	10	··	4	··	3	··	6	··	5	··	4	··	11	6	Neal
16	··	4	··	6	··	9	··	7	··	4	··	3	··	3	··	6	··	7	Gill
12	··	6	··	13	··	4	··	17	··	7	··	9	··	16	··	8	··	8	Carlthorpe
··	10	··	6	··	12	··	11	··	4	··	9	··	10	··	5	··	15	9	Matthews
6	··	9	··	7	··	10	··	12	··	9	··	5	··	11	··	17	··	10	Plant
··	17	··	15	··	13	··	9	··	10	··	7	··	6	··	8	··	5	11	Topham
··	2	··	1	··	2	··	1	··	2	··	1	··	2	··	1	··	2	12	Brackenbury
7	··	14	··	9	··	8	··	6	··	10	··	7	·	14	··	4	··	13	Broster
4	··	16	··	8	··	12	··	10	··	6	··	13	··	15	··	14	··	14	Porter
9	··	15	··	10	··	7	··	13	··	8	··	17	··	4	··	16	··	15	Ranshaw on Trial
··	9	··	7	··	14	··	16	··	6	··	15	··	12	··	17	··	9	16	Walkley do
14	··	18	··	15	··	18	··	14	··	18	··	15	··	8	··	18	··	17	Dunington do
																		18	Kirk do

Did not go to Stessing

proper Substitute.   No Place **must** be neglected.

SPILSBY.

LINCOLNSHIRE METHODISM

FRONT COVER: John Wesley preaching over his father's grave at
Epworth. (DNR)

Statuette of John Wesley.

LINCOLNSHIRE METHODISM

Celebrating 250 years

BY

WILLIAM LEARY BA

BARRACUDA BOOKS LIMITED
BUCKINGHAM, ENGLAND
MCMLXXXVIII

PUBLISHED BY
BARRACUDA BOOKS LIMITED
BUCKINGHAM, ENGLAND
AND PRINTED BY
EBENEZER BAYLIS & SON LIMITED
WORCESTER, ENGLAND

BOUND BY
HUNTER & FOULIS LTD
EDINBURGH, SCOTLAND

JACKET PRINTED BY
CHENEY & SONS LIMITED
BANBURY, OXON

PHOTOLITHOGRAPHY BY
SOUTH MIDLANDS LITHOPLATES LTD
LUTON, ENGLAND

TYPESETTING BY
QUILL AUTOGRAPHICS LIMITED
BANBURY, ENGLAND

ISBN 0 86023 421 5

Contents

Introduction

I was born and brought up in Lincolnshire and lived in the county until the outbreak of the Second World War. After the war and training in a Methodist College, I was ordained in the Methodist Ministry in 1949. While many years have been spent away from Lincolnshire, I have always loved the people and places. Over the years much material has been collected — copious notes on all the chapels in every town and village, thousands of references to people and events, statistics and dates and photographs. All this accumulated material has made it possible at last to produce a book of this kind.

I have tried to show the events through the years — the courage of the first Methodists against much opposition, their intrepidity in pioneering causes, their skills in preaching and teaching and their outreach into the wider community, as well as the building of chapels. To do this, original sources of minute books, preaching plans and journals have been used, as well as contemporary newspapers and magazines.

My debt is to a number of people. Rex Russell of Barton upon Humber provided a handlist of relevant items culled from the *Lincoln, Rutland and Stamford Mercury*, thus making it easier to locate material from that paper. His extensive work on Methodist day and Sunday schools has been a worthy contribution to this aspect of Methodist history, and for that reason I have not written at length on these.

Illustrations have come from a variety of sources, and acknowledgement is made of those used from other collections, many from kind friends.

Above all my grateful thanks go to David Robinson for reading the manuscript and making valuable suggestions, detecting errors, supplying further illustrations from his extensive Lincolnshire collection, and for his expert guidance in preparing for publication.

Key to Caption Credits

BL	Mrs B. Lidgett	LCL	Lincoln City Libraries
BR	Bert Rawlings	LE	Laurence Elvin
DG	Dennis Gilbert	LEC	Miss L. E. Cussons
DNR	David N. Robinson	LS	Mrs Lydia Skipworth
GJ	Grantham Journal	OT	Mrs O. Townsend
HJ	H. Jubbs	PHR	Philip H. Race
HL	Mrs Hazel Lawson	WC	W. Coulam
HS	Miss Harriet Sanderson		all others from the author's collection.

Foreword

By Rev Dr John A. Newton

The Reverend William Leary is well-known as a Methodist historian and archivist. He is peculiarly well equipped to write this study of Methodism in Lincolnshire, from its eighteenth-century origins to the present day. He is, first, a son of Lincolnshire himself, and understands its people. Furthermore, having served as the Connexional Archivist for Methodism, he has an unrivalled knowledge of first-hand sources. He introduces his readers to the fascinating primary sources of Methodist history — diaries, letters, circuit plans, circuit minute books, Quarter Sessions Rolls, and episcopal Visitation Returns.

Again, Mr Leary is an historian who knows Methodist history on the ground, so to say. He has not only spent thirty years in study and research in his chosen field. He has also taken to heart that salutary advice that there comes a time for the historian to lay aside his books, and put on his boots. He has walked the ground, travelled the county, visited the circuits, and inventoried its chapels from personal acquaintance.

Lincolnshire will always have a special fascination for Methodists, as the home of the Wesleys. For over two centuries, moreover, it has been, like Cornwall and County Durham, Methodist heartland. Mr Leary quotes Wesley on the people of Lincoln City as having, 'Not much fire and vigour of spirit, perhaps more mildness and gentleness'. There is truth in that judgement, though by no means the whole truth. What they lack in obvious 'fire', the Lincolnshire people make up in dogged loyalty and devotion. Those qualities surely, humanly speaking, help to explain Wesley's enthusiastic verdict of 1761: 'I find the work of God increases on every side, but particularly in Lincolnshire, where there has been no work like this since the time I preached on my father's tomb.'

That expansion and revival was no nine days' wonder. It bred a Methodist tradition of Christian discipleship which produced men of the calibre of Richard Watson, John Hunt of Fiji, Thomas Jackson, Henry Bett, Robert Perks, and Henry Lunn. Mr Leary chronicles them all; but his real heroes are the preachers, class leaders, stewards, and members: the people called Methodists.

Here is a book to read both for enlightenment and for pleasure. Mr Leary has put us in his debt by writing it with such knowledge and affection.

John A. Newton

Preface

By Rev Dr John A. Harrod MA, BSc

I am delighted and privileged to be asked to write this preface, first, because of a long standing association between William Leary and my family. He and my father were colleagues in the Lincoln North Methodist Circuit some thirty years ago — the former as minister and the latter as circuit steward. The author did in fact conduct my confirmation in 1961. Secondly, it was within Lincolnshire Methodism that I was nurtured. The resilience of its chapels is shown in the fact that they have survived my first efforts at preaching!

The story of Methodism in Lincolnshire is told here with scholarly skill. It includes the high points — for example the extraordinary sacrificial commitment of the early Methodists. It includes also the low points — for example the reluctance of some churches to effect the union of 1932. Methodism has never been a church yoked to its tradition; but that I hope does not mean we fail to honour the past, or learn and gain inspiration from it. William Leary's fine study will help us to do this.

John A. Harrod

Dedication

to Marie
my wife, who has travelled up
and down the county with me,
sharing this and everything.

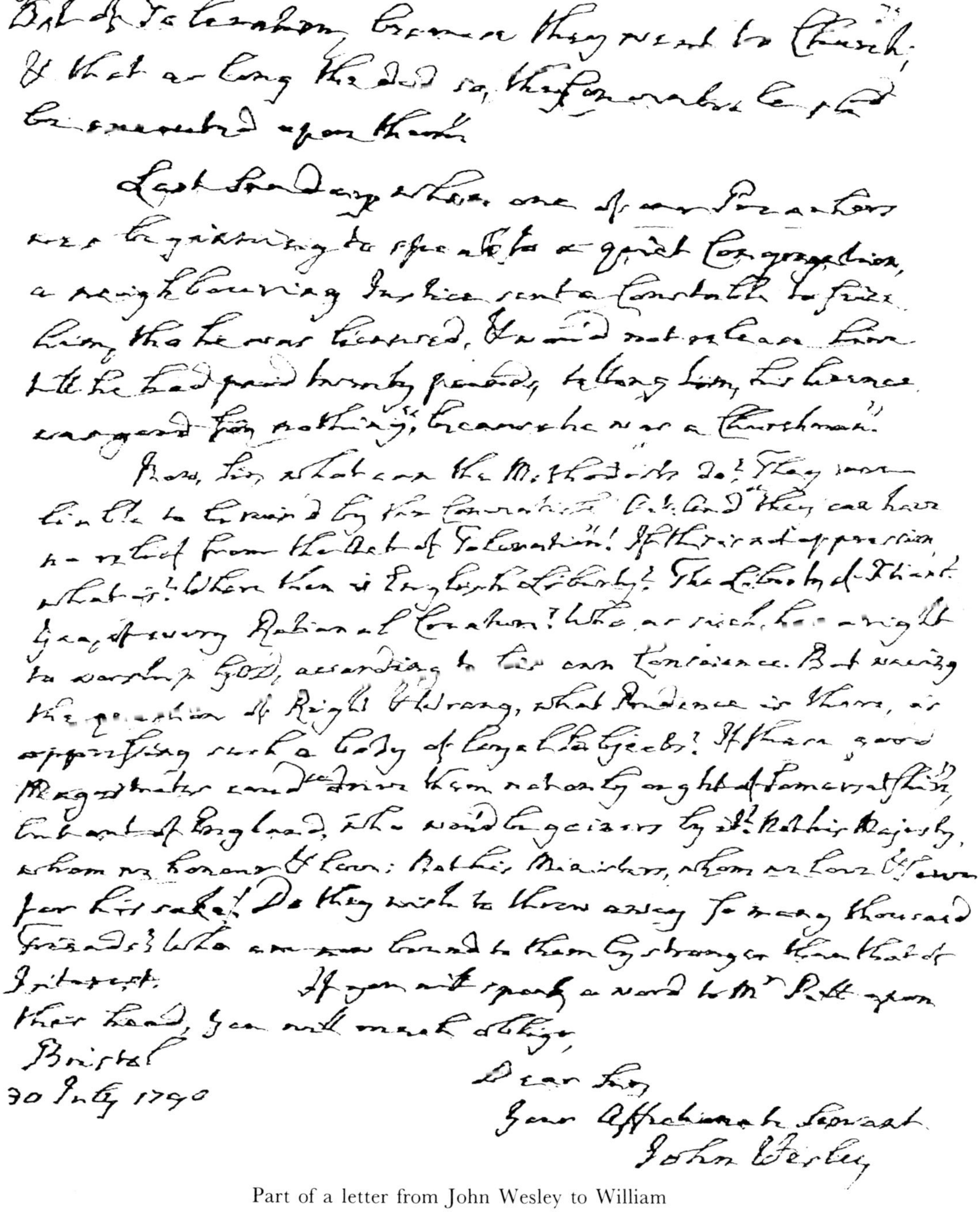
Bill of Toleration because they went to Church;
& that as long they did so, the Five mile Act could not
be executed upon them.

Last Sunday when one of our Preachers
was beginning to speak to a quiet Congregation,
a neighbouring Justice sent a Constable to seize
him, tho he was licensed, & would not release him
till he had paid twenty pounds, telling him, his licence
was good for nothing, "because he was a Churchman."

Now, Sir, what can the Methodists do? They are
liable to be ruined by the "Conventicle Act." And they can have
no relief from the "Act of Toleration"! If this is not oppression,
what is? Where then is English Liberty? The Liberty of Christians,
Yea, of every Rational Creature? Who, as such, has a right
to worship GOD, according to his own Conscience. But waving
the question of Right & Wrong, what Prudence is there, in
oppressing such a body of loyal Subjects? If these good
Magistrates could drive them not only out of Somersetshire,
but out of England, who would be gainers by it? Not his Majesty,
whom we honour & love: Not his Ministers, whom we love & serve
for his sake! Do they wish to throw away so many thousand
Friends? who are now bound to them by stronger ties than that of
Interest. If you will speak a word to Mr Pitt upon
that head, you will much oblige,

Bristol
30 July 1790

Dear Sir,
Your Affectionate Servant
John Wesley

Part of a letter from John Wesley to William Wilberforce, 1790.

John Wesley's escape from the rectory fire, 1709 — the 'brand plucked from the burning'.

John Wesley's Lincolnshire

In 1709 the rectory at Epworth was burnt down. John Wesley was six years old. Some historians believe the fire was started deliberately by angry people in the parish who sought redress against an unwanted person; others relate that the rectory caught fire by the carelessness of Samuel Wesley himself. The story goes that, before he retired for the night, he looked round the house with a lighted candle and held it too close to the thatched roof, starting the conflagration. Fortunately all the family escaped and John was the last to be rescued from the flames. He never forgot that he was a 'brand plucked from the burning'.

It matters not which historian was right. For John Wesley it was a frequent reminder that he had been providentially spared for the most important thing in his life. Having been rescued from the fire he believed he had been saved for a divine mission to all mankind.

John Wesley was born in 1703 and died in 1791. His life therefore covered most of the 18th century, and his work occupied at least half of it. Born into the church with an Anglican as well as Nonconformist background, he was fitted for his future work by a dedicated mother, Susanna, a first class school and a college training. More than his educational achievements, however, was his personal discipline, his warmed heart experience of 24 May 1738, and his deep conviction that he had a special calling to fulfil.

The century was particularly marked for the weakness and lethargy of the Established Church, although locally the Diocese of Lincoln was cared for by some able Bishops and many hard-working clergy. Often the ignorance and ill-manners of the people made the work of the parson difficult. Hetty Wesley, Samuel's daughter, described Wroot as a 'place devoid of wisdom, wit and grace'. Epworth was worse. Samuel Wesley did his best in both parishes, but the people never appreciated his wisdom nor his gifts. 'The Christian faith will surely revive in this kingdom,' he once said to John, 'you will see it though I shall not.'

Although many parsons only celebrated Holy Communion at long intervals, confirmations in the Diocese were quite staggering. In 1709 there were 1,200 confirmations at Grantham, 800 in Lincoln, 600 at Caistor, 500 at Louth, 600 at Horncastle, 1,000 at Boston and 500 at Sleaford. In 1771 Bishop Green confirmed more than 5,000 people in the Diocese.

Nonconformity flourished during the whole of the 18th century, and in many parts of the county there were long established Congregational churches, notably at Sleaford, Gainsborough, Grimsby, Alford and Louth. There were Independent Chapels at Barrow on Humber, Clixby, Spilsby and Friskney; there were Baptist Chapels at Coningsby, Messingham, in the Fens and in the Isle of Axholme.

John Wesley encouraged William Wilberforce in his work, and the agitation for the abolition of the slave trade took practical shape at the dinner table of Bennet Langton, a Lincolnshire gentleman. The Lindsey Quarter Sessions Rolls record how the Justices started a campaign for the better observance of Sunday, and for the reformation of manners and morals, a movement dear to the heart of John Wesley. There was increased concern for prison reform towards the end of the 18th century and Wesley inspired John Howard in his campaign. The new prison at Spilsby, built in 1775, contained a surgery, bathroom and fumigating room. In 1786 the keeper of the Lincoln prison prohibited the sale of beer to the prisoners.

Meetings were held in Lincoln in 1786 with the intention of founding a hospital; the following year the County Hospital was established. Early in the 19th century, institutions for mental patients were opened at Horncastle and Lincoln.

Lincolnshire was then, as now, a predominantly agricultural county with broad acres of corn and root crops, but there were other industries too. There was a thriving wool trade, cloth was woven at Waltham and Bolingbroke, hemp at Haxey, flax at Epworth, Belton had its 'flax fair' and there was a linseed mill at Gainsborough. The development of the ports and watering places came in the next century.

The 19th century saw a tremendous surge in industrial expansion with the coming of the railways, the gas companies, the developments of the ports of Boston, Gainsborough and Grimsby. Provision was made for the educational improvement of the working classes in the establishment of the Mechanics' Institutes, the Literary Societies, and the opening of libraries. In 1839 there were over a hundred Friendly Societies in the county and sixteen Savings Banks, and these were to increase.

Many of the early Methodists were agricultural labourers, but there were many tenant farmers too, whose names appear on many Methodist Property Deeds. In the towns, Methodists composed a large cross-section of trades — artisans, shop-keepers, professional people, besides many who were Justices of the Peace and town councillors, including Mayors.

Methodism was rooted in the county in the early 1740s and, within thirty years, there were Methodist groups in most of the towns of Lindsey and Holland, and nearly half the villages. Kesteven was considerably later in setting up Methodist societies. By the end of the 18th century there were forty preaching places of sorts, or improvised rooms, and close on 250 societies. The number was doubled in the next fifty years.

The establishment of Methodist societies was the result of Wesley's influence, but it is debatable whether in fact he actually brought people together in what became the first distinctively Methodist groups. His visits to Lincolnshire were spaced at two year intervals and he concentrated on Epworth, visiting his birthplace on every occasion, but in other towns and villages his visits were little more than sporadic and uneventful.

Although Wesley formed no society directly himself, yet he met those which had been formed, speaking privately with members, removing difficulties, and encouraging those who were the leaders. He found on some occasions the people were rude and wild, but others receptive and placid. His comment on the people of Lincoln city may well constitute his judgement on Lincolnshire people generally: 'Not much fire and vigour of spirit, perhaps more mildness and gentleness'.

Wesley had great admiration for Lincoln cathedral in both style and position; he took a look at the old castle at Tattershall and found pleasure in visiting the old baronial hall at Gainsborough. He climbed Boston Stump when he was seventy-seven years old. The only remaining chapel in the county which he opened is at Raithby, near Spilsby, and still used. But the rectory at Epworth is a permanent link with those days and with Methodism's founder. Appropriately, his last visit to the county was to his old home, when he preached in the market place 'to such a congregation as was never seen at Epworth before'.

ABOVE: Susanna Wesley, wife of Samuel. BELOW: Rev Samuel Wesley.
Rector of Epworth (1697-1735). CENTRE: Birthplace of John Wesley.
(DNR)

15

ABOVE: John Wesley, after a painting by G. Romney, 1789. BELOW:
Tattershall Castle, a Lincolnshire landmark visited by John Wesley.

ABOVE: Charles Wesley, aged 76. LEFT: Boston Stump, climbed by
Wesley at the age of 77. (DNR) BELOW: Lincoln College, Oxford, of which
John Wesley was elected a fellow in 1726.

Market Cross in Epworth from which Wesley preached.

Beginnings

When John Wesley and John Taylor, his travelling companion, rode into Epworth on 5 June 1742, it was for Wesley a return home, yet a home in many ways different from that which he had left some years before. His father had been dead for seven years, and his mother was living in London; she died less than three weeks later. Not only was Epworth different; Wesley too was a changed man. Since that spring day in 1735 when the family had stood round the grave of old Samuel, John and Charles had been to Georgia; both had experienced a conversion which had changed their spiritual outlook; John, more than Charles, had begun travelling around the country, setting up Methodist headquarters at London and Bristol. Already he had been as far north as Newcastle.

Back home, Wesley enquired of the landlord of the Red Lion inn if there were folk in the town who might 'not be ashamed of my acquaintance'. Wesley appeared to be in haste, but he stayed the night in the town and, on the following morning, the church was crowded in expectation of hearing him preach. Instead, the people listened to Mr Romley, the curate, preach on the dangers of 'enthusiasm'. Not to be outdone, Wesley preached in the evening from his father's tombstone, and then went to the house of Edward Smith, where he met a number of people from the nearby villages. Says Wesley, 'all desired that I would come over to help them', and the urgency of the request compelled him to stay in Epworth several days.

There was no official appointment of Wesley's preachers until 1765, but before that a number of men had joined him and were travelling around the country. Thomas Meyrick spent a short time in Epworth in 1747 and thenceforth others came for brief periods. One of the earliest to come to Grimsby was John Nelson, the stonemason from Birstall, and Alexander Mather, a Scotsman who fought at Culloden, had a roving commission which included Epworth, Gainsborough, Grimsby and Sheffield. His companions in the work were Thomas Tobias, Thomas Hanby and Thomas Lee. Lee explains the plan of labour: 'I spent two months on the eastern side of the county, preaching in different places, and superintending the affairs of the little societies; and then two months on the west'. There were months when the societies had no preacher at all.

The progress of the movement was not without many occasions of opposition. The curate of Epworth refused the early Methodists the privileges of the church and the sacraments. Wesley faced violence in a number of towns and villages. At Crowle in 1748 the 'wild congregation' forced him to seek protection in the garden of George Stovin, a Justice of the Peace. What safer place indeed! In 1743 John Nelson faced a mob when taking his stand on a table near William Blow's house in Grimsby. 'As I was preaching', he says, 'the minister and three men came to play quoits, as near the people as they could get; but with all their playing and shouting they could not draw anyone from hearing'. When he visited the town six months later 'the minister got a man to beat the town drum . . . and went before the drum, and gathered all the rabble he could, giving them liquor to go with him to fight for the church . . . ' When Nelson finished preaching, the mob attacked in earnest. They smashed the windows of Blow's house, tore up pavings in the streets, broke stanchions and furniture. The following morning the drummer returned and furiously beat his drum for an hour but, proving ineffective in the face of Nelson's preaching, the drummer listened and, before the end, was converted. Says Nelson: 'We had great peace in our shattered house that night'.

There were 'rude and noisy crowds' when Wesley visited Grimsby in 1745 and, two years after, Charles Wesley fared no better. He was grabbed by the mob on entering the town and prevented from preaching out of doors. The rabble invaded the room, but the masculine superiority of William Blow resulted in the room being cleared and Wesley preached in peace.

At Waltham the home of William Robinson was opened for preaching. The folk who gathered were often disturbed by ruffians, who beat kettles outside while services were being held. On one occasion while Thomas Carlill was preaching, 'some filthy fellow threw among the people some sheep's puddings; and at another time, a person flung a hive of bees amongst them'. Wesley preached at Laceby to a congregation both quiet and earnest but, some time afterwards, when Thomas Tomlinson opened his house for services, the local farmer took umbrage on the grounds that the few who met had to pass by a bridge close to his corn stacks. Their lighted lanterns were a fire hazard, and so the farmer removed the bridge in an attempt to stop the meetings, but all he succeeded in doing was to transfer the place of meeting to John Scrivener's mill at Aylesby.

At North Thoresby, William Burman, a farmer, fitted up one of his stables for meetings, and soon the mob attacked the improvised conventicle. 'Sometimes they fumigated the place where they assembled with the odour of asafoetida; at other times through a hole in the window they syringed blood upon them, and often cut their coats and garments with scissors'. Richard Boardman, later a pioneer in American Methodism, had on one occasion to apply to the magistrates at Louth for redress, and not without success, for the persecutors were dealt with and peace restored, with the church bells rung to celebrate the Methodist victory.

When Wesley first visited Barrow on Humber he was attacked by the mob, but 'as more and more of the angry ones came within hearing, they lost all their fierceness'. At Barton upon Humber, when Wesley arrived from Hull with 'two such brutes as I have seldom seen', the local people mustered with a large wagon rope and, with a horse at each end, gently drew the preacher and people out of the town. Robert Costerdine, another of Wesley's preachers, relates how the people of South Ferriby met him like roaring lions.

Wesley encountered many 'adversaries stirred up by a bad man' at Scotter. Riots followed his visit and the magistrate had to be called in to quell the mob. The vicar of Caistor took exception to Methodist prayer meetings, and an altercation ensued between a few pious women and the vicar. When Robert Carr Brackenbury, the squire of Raithby Hall, came to Caistor to preach, it was his own brother Richard, a captain in the army, who led the opposition, which took the form of directing a drummer and fife to move into the crowd during the preaching. The sequel to that was the conversion of Richard himself.

Wesley described the town of Louth as 'formerly a den of lions', but that was shortlived. At Horncastle, 'Satan's children threatened terrible things', and it was the vicar who rose in indignation at the presence of the Methodists in the town, and called a meeting at the Bull Hotel to decide how best to get rid of them. 'Ministers', he said, 'are raving enthusiasts, pretending to divine impulse, and thus have obtained sway among the ignorant'.

Daniel Jackson, an itinerant preacher, received some rough handling at Wainfleet, but hardly any record surpassses that of Thomas Mitchell, another itinerant, who visited Wrangle in 1752. He preached out of doors while constables, followed by a mob, approached the scene. Mitchell himself tells the story at length in vivid detail. 'They violently broke in upon the people, siezed me, pulled me down, and took me to the public house, where they kept me till four in the afternoon'. At the instigation of the vicar, Mitchell was brought out, thrown into a pond, and 'several times I strove to get out, but they pitched me in again'. After this rough treatment the mob covered him all over with paint and took him again to the public house. 'Here I was kept, till they put five of our friends into the water. Then they came and took me out again, and carried me to a great pond . . . and threw me as far as they could into the water'. The dreadful record goes on. He was eventually put to bed by some kind friend, but soon the mob came and brought him into the street, forcing a promise that he would never again return to the village. Mitchell concludes: 'In the midst of this persecution, many were brought to the saving knowledge of God'.

Thomas Mitchell and Alexander Mather preached in the market place at Boston and much the same treatment was meted to them both: 'dirt and stones flew like hail on every side'. The preachers were manhandled, but they managed to get to an inn, and then the landlord was threatened for giving them shelter. It was more than a year before both recovered from the onslaught of the mob. John Hannah, a young man from Glentworth, met opposition in Lincoln, so much so that he died as a direct result of mob violence. In the village of Newton upon Trent, Caroline Skelton opened her house for preaching, but at great risk to herself and those who came there for worship. The mob 'broke all the windows to shivers. Next they went to the stable, and cutting the mane and tail of the preacher's horse, proceeded to tar and cover it with feathers'.

Another brave woman was Mrs Watkinson of Navenby who, having taken in Baptist preachers, suffered in consequence at the hands of the mob. She then entertained the Calvinist preachers with the same result. Robert Cresswell suffered similarly in the same village, and then William Hazard housed the society, but his fellow farmers destroyed his property and supplied drinks to the rabble by way of reward. When Thomas Emery opened his house in Great Gonerby, the meetings were constantly interrupted and people assaulted as they left the house. Emery was the village baker and depended on the farmers to cart the wood and fuel; as a reprisal for his Methodist allegiance they withdrew the use of the horses or put objects in their pathway.

People risked a great deal when they opened their homes for Methodist meetings or gave support to the preaching. Some risked ejection. Benjamin Pearson, a poor labouring man at Limber, was turned out of his house because he allowed preaching, but even this did not deter him from going to the home of James Roe and sharing in Methodist worship there. Thomas Basker of Ashby by Partney became the self-appointed leader of a small class and invited Wesley to his house, knowing all the time that he was held in suspicion by his landlord. 'The principal person in the village, whose tenants we were, having long beheld the Methodists with an evil eye, determined, at last, to rid himself of them by ejecting them out of their places. He sent his servants to take observation of such as frequented the private meetings'. Basker was turned out of his house.

John Mayfield of Boothby was tenant to a local farmer. John was converted in the improvised chapel at Gowt's Bridge in Lincoln and returned home to put his newfound faith into practice. He was soon shepherd of a few earnest Methodists, but at once put himself and his home in jeopardy. He too was threatened with ejection. The conspirators were sure they would succeed in getting John discharged, when they informed the steward that John had made the house in which he lived a conventicle. When the time came for the preaching, the steward expressed a wish to hear him, requesting the farmers to accompany him, but he was so impressed with what he heard that all charges were withdrawn. By 1806 there were 68 members on Mayfield's class book; the population of the hamlet was hardly more.

Opposition from the clergy, mob violence, ejection by landlords — these were some of the difficulties which the early Methodists faced in many parts of the county. But neither persecution nor the risk of ejection deterred the Methodists from seeking the help of Wesley and his preachers. Edward Holmes, schoolmaster and class leader at Wroot, appealed to Jasper Robinson, the Superintendent at Epworth, to come and assist him, 'assuring him that the hearts and homes of the people were open to receive him and his colleagues with all readiness of mind'. Something of the fervour and intrepidity of those early leaders is shown in the case of William Blow of Grimsby who, with a boy, walked all the way from his home to Epworth to invite Wesley to come to Grimsby. Wesley sent John Nelson, an acceptable substitute as it turned out, and the long walk was with the satisfaction that help was forthcoming. The keeper of the courthouse at Lincoln invited Wesley in when a storm threatened to mar the outdoor preaching. Sir Nevil Hickman opened the Old Hall at Gainsborough to the preaching, and himself being personally present thanked Wesley for his sermon. Gentry at Alford 'desired me to preach in the market place'.

Wesley went to Cleethorpes for the first time in 1781, when already there was a society numbering forty, with William Robinson as the leader, and whose house had been registered for meetings for more than twenty years. Wesley says, 'I could not go into any of the little houses, or they would not be satisfied. Several of these are clearly renewed in love, and give a plain, scriptural account of their experience'.

Religious societies were in some instances a mixture of several brands of theological belief. Many of the so-called Methodist societies were in fact a mixture of Independents, Calvinists and Methodists. Such a group met in Barton upon Humber in 1760, in the house of Thomas Lutys, who lived in Market Lane, now King Street. Twenty years passed before a licence was issued for a house distinctly Methodist. There was a Calvinistic congregation at Barrow on Humber and Methodist work was slow to take root in consequence. When Wesley visited Grimsby in 1779 he gave frank expression of his opinion of the Calvinistic preachers in the town. 'I found a little trial. In this, and many others parts of the kingdom, these striplings who call themselves Lady Huntingdon's preachers have greatly hindered the work of God. They have neither sense, courage, nor grace to go up and beat the devil's quarters in any place where Christ has been named; but wherever we have entered, as by storm, and gathered a few souls, often at the peril of our lives, they creep in and, by doubtful disputations, set everyone's sword against his brother'.

The congregation at Sir Nevil Hickman's hall may not all have been Methodists, for in 1773 'a large room in the old hall' was licensed under the name of John Fletcher, a grocer in the town, and from this stemmed a group under the name of the Countess of Huntingdon. This body soon had a chapel erected in Mr Dean's yard and in 1781 Wesley preached there, knowing his company to be mixed, but all 'seemed much affected'.

Numerous licences obtained by individuals for private homes point to a variety of nonconformist groups, none of which in these early days can be described as distinctly Methodist, although from many of them Methodist societies emerged.

OPPOSITE: Gainsborough Old Hall, where Wesley preached. ABOVE: Gainsborough's first chapel (c1774). RIGHT: Mrs Fisher's house in Meanwell Court, Lincoln, the first Methodist chapel in the city, visited by Wesley in 1790. (DNR) BELOW: Red Lion Inn at Epworth where Wesley stayed once.

ABOVE: John Nelson (1707-1774), one of the first preachers to go to Grimsby. CENTRE: Alexander Mather, who preached in the market place at Boston. BELOW: Wesley House, Winterton, where John preached. RIGHT: Dissenting Certificate (1807) for a private house in Broxholme.

THESE are to certify whom it may concern, that a Certificate bearing Date the _twenty fifth_ Day of _October_ in the Year of our Lord, One Thousand, Eight Hundred, and _seven_ under the Hands of _Thomas Chalner John Gray and George Boole_

certifying that a certain _Dwelling House in the Occupation of John Gray_

Broxholm situate in the Parish of in the County and Diocese of Lincoln, is intended to be used as a Place of religious Worship, for those of His Majesty's Protestant Subjects dissenting from the Church of England, commonly called Methodists, was registered in the Registry of the Lord Bishop of Lincoln, this _fourteenth_ Day of _November_ in the Year of our Lord One Thousand Eight Hundred, and _seven_

Witness my Hand,

John Fardell

Depty. Regr. of the Diocese of Lincoln

People Called Methodists

The progress of Methodism depended more and more upon the local people, many of whom had heard Wesley preach, or had come into the Methodist stream by hearing one of his preachers. Important to most was their sense of spiritual need and the desire to satisfy that need in corporate prayer or meetings of exhortation. Self-appointed leaders came forward with no other authority save the strong conviction that it was expedient. Immature many of them were, but they gathered like-minded people to their homes, and in this way many societies were started, supported only occasionally by travelling preachers.

Unfortunately, the reports of these local pioneers is fragmentary, but those which exist are illuminating, and testify to the sense of urgency which men and women had for their neighbours' spiritual welfare. Thomas Meyrick was one of Wesley's travelling preachers, but in a brief note to Wesley in 1747, he corrects the supposition that everything went well once a society was in existence: 'at Grimsby all is peacable, but I found the society all broken in pieces; they had no public or private meetings for almost two months, and the leaders have left the town to get work, and there is neither man nor woman that seem anyway qualified for that office'.

So much depended on local leadership. When Wesley went to Tetney in 1747 he examined the little society. 'I have not seen such another in England. In the class paper . . . I observed one gave eightpence, often 10d, a week; another 13, 15 or 18d; another one, sometimes two shillings. I asked Micah Elmoor, the leader "How is this? Are you the richest society in England?" He answered, "I suppose not; but all of us who are single persons agreed together, to give both ourselves, and all we have to God: and we do it gladly; whereby we are able from time to time to entertain all the strangers that come to Tetney, who often have no food to eat, nor any friend to give them lodgings". After Elmoor's death the cause ceased and was not revived until Thomas Ludlam, a labourer, did so.

Jonathan Robinson, father of William, (both were carpenters), was the first leader at Waltham and when he died in 1763 there was fortunately a succession of leaders for forty years, but then the cause ceased. It was always doubtful whether a society once started could be maintained, for success and growth always depended upon some leader being there at the right time. At Great Coates William Butters made a start in his own home in 1759, and for forty years the cause was sustained because three or four able men succeeded him.

The insular nature of village life tended towards an insular society; people seldom travelled far, particularly villagers, for they had little time left for social intercourse when work was done. It was also a risky business travelling in winter. There are numerous tales of Methodist preachers having precarious journeys and arriving home late due to an accident with pony and trap. The growing awareness of Methodism as a connexional system led, slowly perhaps, to a leader or preacher going beyond the bounds of his own village or two to some more distant place. Indeed, it was a person's allegiance to Methodism which made him mobile, and sent him off to his neighbours, either to pioneer a new cause or foster one already in existence. It was this unity of purpose and the sense of fellowship which became part of the spiritual awakening, which in turn led people to go to the next village.

Anthony Kemp and Jane Bromley went from their home at Keelby to Habrough to hear a Methodist preacher, and in turn they invited the preacher to their village. Neither of them could lead a class, so they resorted to Riby and invited Thomas Catley to come and help. Matthew Cunningham of Scartho was a man of independent means and able therefore to devote much time to helping societies; already he was a preacher of good standing. He went to Beelsby and set up a class of eleven people in his brother's mill. There was preaching at Barnoldby le Beck in the house of Edward Abey, a farmer, but when Abey left the village it ceased, until Cunningham brought them together again and appointed Cornelius Hewson as leader. George Laming of Tetney went to Holton le Clay and asked Thomas Wilson to help. These two organised a link between the two villages, and united fellowship continued for years. Laming went to Humberston and took with him Stephen Noddall, and they met in the house of Joseph Richardson. But Richardson was already attached to the Cleethorpes society, and so a link was forged between his own people in Humberston and those in Cleethorpes.

The circuit system emerged, for people were mixing together as they had never done before; they had something to talk about and a message to hear. It soon became apparent that when a Methodist moved house he took his newfound religion with him, and gathered people in a new home. William Tomlinson, a farmer who came to reside at Humberston from Yorkshire was a preacher and leader, and that gave a boost to the society which Richardson had left. George Houghton was another farmer at Killingholme and started Methodism there, and then went to live at East Halton and repeated the good work. He himself had been brought into touch with Methodism in Winterton and, after moves to Ferriby and Elsham, he settled at Wrawby and invited preachers to his home, whence sprang Methodism in Brigg. Another Yorkshireman, George Stephenson, came to Elsham, set up business as a carpenter and became a preacher, 'and such was his pious concern for the good of the cause, and the accommodation for the servants of God; and he left in his Will several generous legacies, that preaching might be supported at Elsham'.

John Bishop first introduced Methodism into Susworth; he was a member of the society for fifty years, and most of that time a class leader and preacher. He travelled each week to Scotter and set up a class there. Edward Wilson of South Somercotes travelled to Grainthorpe. He and his brother, a schoolmaster at Fotherby, traversed the villages around and it was Edward who set up eight members in Grainthorpe in 1772; by 1798 the group had increased to seventy with a chapel to house them. Jonathan Hay invited preachers to his farmhouse at Great Carlton, becoming the leader, with eight members which rose to nearly sixty in fifteen years. He did similar work at South Reston and, when he retired to Louth, it was to devote his years to producing a house for ministers.

Henry Woodford was a shepherd and later a farmer. He was converted at Saltfleet, became a class leader, when his master declared he would have no Methodist as a tenant, and gave him the option to quit or cease attending Methodist meetings. Woodford stood firm and in the end convinced his master that honesty did pay and was rewarded by retaining his job.

Langham Row, in the Lincolnshire Marsh near Mumby, was never more than a hamlet, but in spite of its obscurity Wesley found it — found it because George Robinson lived there with his nineteen children, a congregation in one family. People from all the villages around came to Langham Row to meet Robinson and hear him preach. Regular services were held in his farmhouse. When Wesley came the congregation 'from many parts, drank in every word'. He came more than once when 'such a multitude flocked together that I was obliged to preach abroad . . . I do not wonder that this society is the largest in these parts of Lincolnshire'.

Robinson erected an octagon chapel next to his granary, and such was the company that flocked to it that it was enlarged twice in the next eighteen years. There were sixty members when Wesley came to 'this lively spot' in 1788, an indication that the marsh folk hungered for the gospel, and braved the east winds to get to the place where it was proclaimed.

William Lambe of Auburn Hall was persuaded to allow a preaching service in the house of one of his tenants. He came to the service himself, and presently twelve members joined together to form a class. The squire became the first class leader, and 'the class prospered in his hands till the day of his death'. His son of the same name continued the good work and gave the first chapel.

Few men made a more permanent impact on their locality than Amos Appleyard of Cleethorpes. Born in 1750 of a fisherman father, he became an apprenticed shoemaker to William Blow of Grimsby. Even with a Methodist master, Amos was not moved to join the society immediately but, when he was converted and set up home in Wardell Street (afterwards called Amos Square), he opened his house to all who wished to hear the preachers. His domestic life was interesting! Twice married, he had eighteen children, and was a grandfather when his last child was born. He became renowned for his prayers, so much so that a revival in the town in 1791 is attributed to his efficacy and zeal.

There were others, many of them farm labourers, shopkeepers, blacksmiths, and carpenters. Most of the local trades were represented among the first class leaders and preachers. Many of them devoid of learning, they nevertheless grasped the importance of the movement and inspired their own folk to respond to the call of the gospel. Most of the societies established in the 18th century were the product of local people — people who could not utter anything in public until they started using their voices in exhortation or prayer. And there were women too.

Robert Blow's wife, Elizabeth, became a member of the society at Grimsby and she crossed the Humber and commenced meetings in Hull. With Elizabeth Simpson and Mary Wilkinson she walked to North Thoresby and started prayer meetings there. They also walked to Caistor and dared to do the same in the open air. Hannah Greetham, a widow, was the first class leader at Wold Newton. When Elizabeth Cook lived in Ravendale she walked the fourteen miles to Grimsby for the 5 am service and, during the week, walked either to Waltham or Binbrook to meet in class. Her husband, Edward Cook, died in 1771 and the following year she married Joseph Richardson of Humberston and with less travel continued her good work.

Mary Barritt, who married Rev Zachariah Taft, was as noble as any woman. She had extraordinary gifts at speaking, missioning the villages of Tetford and Billinghay and the towns of Boston and Spilsby. At Langham Row under her ministry there was 'a flame of fire'. Her usefulness continued under her new name and she worked in Grimsby with tremendous success.

Strangely Methodism did not arrive in the city of Lincoln until 1787, when Sarah Parrot walked from Bracebridge along the old Roman road to Sturton by Stow and met a class there. She often wondered how Methodism might be brought to Lincoln, and the Sturton folk felt it could be done if some good Methodist would go and live there. The name of Mrs Fisher was mentioned, but she lived at Great Gonerby. So the bold Sarah Parrot walked from Lincoln to Great Gonerby to put the question to her. Dorothy Fisher was a widow of means and had been instrumental in bringing Methodism to Gonerby, and the society there had been blessed by her gifts and her bounty. When she heard the request she responded by moving house to Meanwell Court in Lincoln. That was the beginning. Soon her house was crowded with people and, when it became too small, they moved into the yard. Lancelot Harrison, the Minister at Gainsborough, came to help and in January 1788 Wesley wrote to Harrison expressing his joy at what had been started: 'I am glad sister Fisher is settled in Lincoln, and that you have begun preaching there again. Hitherto it has been "a soil ungrateful to the tiller's toils", and possibly it may bear fruit'.

It did. Soon a room was fitted up at Gowt's Bridge and Dorothy Fisher arranged a regular preaching service. Differences of social class are evident in the origin of the cause and future

27

Raithby chapel, opened by Wesley 1 July 1779.

generations have not been allowed to forget, for a tablet set up in the Wesley Chapel in 1836, tells how 'Sarah Parrot, a woman of Bracebridge, and Mrs Fisher, a lady of Gonerby' were instrumental in the hands of God in the introduction of Methodism in this city.

The cause was well established in Grantham when Ellen Gretton, a clergyman's daughter, came to the town and set up a milliner's business. She had many trials once she committed herself to the Methodist society, not least the rejection from her own home and the loss of an annuity. But she stood her ground, married William Christian of Skillington, and started speaking in public — 'and the Lord approved of what she did in this way may be inferred from the general acceptance with which her labours of love were met, and the extensive profit which was consequent upon her exertions'. Ellen went to Sleaford and did similar work there.

Ann Christian of Skillington has been described as 'the belle of the village' and she rode a horse with admired agility. Her conversion led to her becoming the first Methodist in her own village and, when a number of farmers espoused the cause, it grew swiftly in a few years. Mary Kerry, lived at Normanton and was led to look out 'for pasturage where her hungry soul might feed.' Pasturage found, she invited the preachers to her home and for thirty years that was the 'chapel'.

Mary Winn of Nettleham housed the first class in her home, moved to Scothern three miles away and repeated the work there. And there were still more. Many houses were registered for protection in the name of the womenfolk, such as Elizabeth Greenfield of Goulceby, Mary Wright of Scotton and Mary Hitchins of Keadby. In many instances women's names appear first in the class books before their husbands, indicating that they preceded their menfolk in membership in society.

Thus it began, small and feeble perhaps in origin, but the first generation of Methodists set up societies, licensed their houses, and nurtured each other in the faith by exhortation and prayer.

Collections from the Several Societies for the Building of the New Room at Grimsby, June 16. 1756.

		£	s	d
1756				
June 16	Recd from Tetney Society	1	4	0
	Recd from Lowbrough Society & Binbrook	4	15	6
	Eliz.th Thompson & Rob.t Leerby 5 each	.	10	.
	a Friend	.	.	6
	Thos. Cafeter	2	11	6
July 1.	Recd from Cleethorpes Society	.	12	6
	Thomas Dean & Fran.s Dean — 10.6. each	1	1	.
9	John Wright	.	5	.
10	Recd from Silsey's Society	3	3	.
	Recd from Wrangle do	2	.	6
	Recd from Coningsby do	2	8	.
	a friend	.	1	6
	Wm Straton	.	.	5
	Joseph Craft	.	1	6
	a friend unknown	.	3	6
	Wm Robinson of Thorpe	.	4	6
	a friend	.	5	.
	Wm Alcood, 5. and a friend 5.	.	10	.
	Mr Wm Draper of Marcus at the Mill	.	15	6
	Recd from Thoresby Society	2	2	.
	Wm Mayler	.	.	5
	Total	24	16	0

Extract from the accounts of Grimsby's first chapel, 1757.

Raithby chapel interior, decorated for a harvest festival. (LS) INSET: Robert Carr Brackenbury, Squire of Raithby Hall, one of Wesley's preachers.

ABOVE: Thomas Jackson, President of the Conference 1838 and 1849.
(DNR) LEFT: Mary Barritt who married Zachariah Taft. RIGHT: Dr
Robert Newton, President of the Conference 1824, 1832, 1840 and 1848.
BELOW: Wesley preaching at a market cross.

ABOVE: Bassingham Wesleyan chapel (1839) and day school. BELOW:
Interior of Epworth old chapel, built 1821.

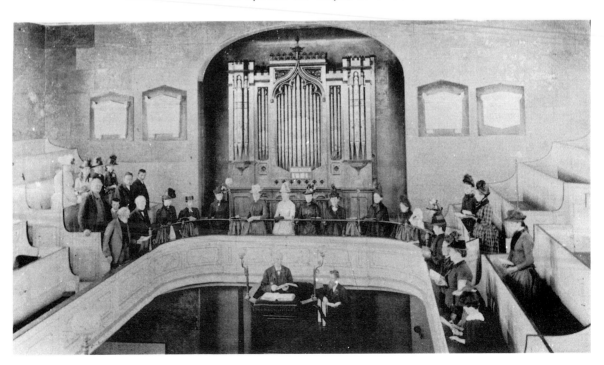

In Barns and Cottages

It is a simple fact that people who heard John Wesley wanted to hear him again, but his visits were sporadic and in some instances he never came again. Instead, the people welcomed his preachers, for they too had a message suited to their needs. Wesley was accustomed to outdoor preaching and so were many of his followers, but what was started in this way soon led to the provision of some room, house or barn. The Dissenting Certificates issued by the Bishop of the Diocese are evidence of the large number of houses or other buildings so registered.

During the 18th century there were something like fifty such certificates issued in respect of what are described as chapels or, to use the current term, meeting houses. These buildings were too fragile to survive more than a generation and it is not known where they stood, nor what they looked like. When, however, a society moved to some other building, that in itself was a mark of progress and advancement. It also afforded larger accommodation and gave the society a sense of status and real promise of continuity.

The claim that the first chapel proper in Lincolnshire was built in Grimsby seems sufficiently authenticated. The prime mover in this venture was Thomas Capitor, a sailor-turned-farmer and a local preacher. He had the co-operation of William Blow, for the chapel was built in Blow's yard in the Bull Ring. It seated 200 people, and John Wesley was there at the opening in 1757. An appeal was made to other Methodists, and places as far distant as Wrangle and Sibsey, and as small as Toft-Newton, contributed to the £78 needed to defray the cost.

Not many places were so swift in securing a place in which to worship. The less able had to be content with a variety of improvised rooms before they were able to build a more permanent chapel. Some of these improvisations were strangely conceived, but no less vital to the society. There was nothing incongruous in moving from a farm kitchen to the out-building, be it a corn granary or a stable. The accommodation was larger, a priority consideration to say the least and, if it was austere, it still afforded shelter from the bad weather. Some of these were licensed for what they were. At Crowle a certificate authorised the use of a 'granary belonging to Richard Anderson in Bank Street in the north end of the town'. At Belton a stable was registered, 'now converted into a chapel, in the occupation of George Cocking'. A stable was used at North Thoresby, and it served the society for forty years. In Haxey and Wroot the Methodists worshipped in the day school.

The first Methodists in Alford secured 'a large building heretofore commonly used as a workshop in the occupation of Thomas Jackson'. After twelve years they moved to 'a certain public building situated in the south end of Alford, the property of William Catley'. Dissenting Certificates bear witness to the types of buildings thus registered. They contain the signatures or marks of local people who made application to the Bishop. There is something quite novel in the reference to 'the new chamber adjoining the corn granary belonging to George Robinson of Langham Row', which was in fact his twice enlarged octagon; or the 'out chamber on the west side of Mr Bell's yard at Laceby'.

But the situation in Grantham offers a rare example of both courage and triumph. Mr Newcomb, an ironmonger who lived in a house next door to the Angel Inn, 'opened a place for the Methodists at the bottom end of a yard, next to back lane, in which they continued for sixteen years. The preaching place was over a smithy, and that not a very large one. The ascent was by a movable ladder, in a narrow passage, leading from the yard into the lane, at the end of the building'. Apparently it was necessary to set a watch during the service in case the ladder was removed. Thomas Cocking, telling the story goes on: 'The value of religion, however, was not diminished by the homliness of the situation thus occupied; nor were the presence of the Saviour and His benefits withholden on that account'. One admires the word 'homliness' in such conditions, especially as the brazier usually made as much noise as he could while the service was in progress. 'His mode of annoyance was to blow the bellows and hammer away on his steady (*sic*) during their occasional meetings for prayer and preaching on weeknights'. In spite of this, the society persisted, and even negotiated the take-over of the whole building, and in fact succeeded when 'all the noisy Vulcanian implements were removed to a situation where their inharmonious sounds became less offensive'.

Behind a number of erections were the efforts and enterprise of many individuals, not all men of property or wealth. The little preaching house at Winterton, still standing, was partly paid for by William Fowler, a youth of sixteen, who gave every penny he had saved towards its erection. Nor was it simply a case of giving money; he became a class leader and sustained that office for thirty years.

One wonders how many chapels were built with an eye to economy, and whether the age of 'do-it-yourself' did not originate among those early Methodists. At South Ferriby, Thomas Waddingham, a farmer, secured 'a parcel of ground commonly called or known by the name of "Cockett Garth", and sought voluntary labour to build the chapel. John Gibson, a joiner, gave his services, while others less skilled did all the labouring. The whole cost only £40 and lasted the society for forty years. George Fowler farmed at Gunhouse and, after his conversion, became an exhorter, later a preacher and, when his native village of East Butterwick was in need of a chapel, he provided the land and paid for the erection. He did the same at Burringham, and also erected one at Gunhouse.

It is now difficult to determine where many of these early buildings stood. The registration certificates define a few. At Spilsby a 'certain chapel or preaching house in a certain yard in the occupation of Robert Martin, near the street called Leather Lane', was opened in 1796. Market Rasen's first chapel was more clearly described, at least as to the location, for it was on land the property of Saul Fox of West Rasen, 'in a street called Jameson Bridge street', and all adjoining landowners are given.

If doubts remain respecting the location of many of the early chapels, there is one 18th century erection about which there is no doubt, and that is the chapel at Raithby, built by the squire, Robert Carr Brackenbury. This architectural gem forms part of the Raithby estate. Having built the fine Hall, Brackenbury added the outbuildings, a stable and, over the stable, the chapel. The entrance is up a stairway, in fact two for, passing through the main door, the stairs branch right and left to meet at the chapel door above. It was opened by Wesley in 1779 and has continued ever since as the only remaining chapel of the period.

Not all landowners were as generously disposed to the Methodists as Squire Brackenbury, but then he was a close friend of Wesley and assisted him in a number of enterprises, most notably in founding Methodism in the Channel Islands. The Methodists were variously criticised in those days, and landowners were, in some instances, suspicious of their activities, but not all, for some provided land for a chapel.

At Great Coates the Methodists were forbidden to build anywhere in the village and for a century they used people's homes. It was late in the next century when the Lord of the Manor, Sir

Richard F. Sutton, granted a piece of land. Francis Sowerby of Aylesby welcomed the Methodists, became one with them, and gave land at both Laceby and Hatcliffe. Many chapels were erected on land with a 99 years' lease, especially those on the estates of Lord Yarborough. When the Methodists at Limber were strong enough to build, they were rather proud of the achievement at having done so near 'the residence of the noble earl', who in any case had given permission.

James Henwood Esq of Hull had grudgingly granted a licence to Benjamin Richardson of Humberston, but grudgingly or otherwise, he later allowed a chapel to be erected. Colonel George Tomlin JP DL gave permission for a chapel to be built at Riby, but went one better — he gave the site out of respect, so it is said, for one of his workmen, Charles Hallett. Mr Grimes was a farmer at Pickworth and had opened his house for preaching and built a room by the side of it, but constructed it in such a way that it had the appearance of a cottage. The local landowner, John Uppleby Esq, recognised the ruse, and so granted a piece of land for a new chapel.

Besides the landowners, there were smallholders and, when once a man had come within the influence of Methodism, there were no bounds to his generosity, exemplified by his readiness to give land and money. Mr Bamford of Owmby was one such. He strove by every possible means to erect a chapel, and succeeded so far as to get bricks and timber and a plot of ground, which was in fact a part of his own garden. Then the good man died and the people of the village despaired of building and sold all the materials. However his daughter Charlotte with her husband, returned to the village, and they set about the building on the original plot of ground and erected the chapel at their own expense.

George Street chapel, Grimsby, 1847. (DNR)

OPENING SERVICES

OF THE

NEW WESLEYAN CHAPEL,

GRIMSBY.

The Public are most respectfully informed that the entire
Services will be held as follow :

On FRIDAY, APRIL 2nd, 1847,

SERMONS

Will be preached in the Forenoon at Half-past Ten, and in the
Evening at Six, by The REV. JOHN LOMAS, of London;
and in the Afternoon at Half-past Two o'clock, by The
REV. W. VEVERS, of Hull.

On SUNDAY, April 4th,

In the Forenoon at Half-past Ten, and in the Evening at Six,
by The REV. A. E. FARRAR, of Sheffield; and in the
Afternoon at Two o'clock, by The REV. H. D. LOWE.

On THURSDAY, April 8th,

In the Afternoon at Half-past Two, and in the Evening at Six,
by The REV. ROBERT NEWTON, D. D.

On SUNDAY, April 11th,

In the Forenoon at Half-past Ten, and in the Evening at Six,
by The REV. J. DOBBIN, LL. D., of Trinity College,
Dublin; and in the Afternoon at Two o'clock, by The REV.
WILLIAM DAWSON.

On TUESDAY, April 13th,

In the Evening at Half-past Six o'clock, by
The REV. JAMES SHERMAN, of Surrey Chapel, London.

On SUNDAY, April 18th,

In the Morning at Half-past Ten, and in the Evening at Six,
by the REV. DR. BEAUMONT, of London; and in the
Afternoon at Two o'clock, by The REV. JAMES LOUTIT.

N.B. DINNER & TEA in the School-rooms, on Friday,
the 2nd, and TEA on Thursday, the 8th of April. Dinner
Tickets, *Two Shillings*—*Ten Tickets, One Shilling* each. *Dinner
and Tea Ticket*, on the 2nd of April, *Two Shillings and Sixpence.*

TICKETS may be had of Mr. SHEPHERD, Grocer—Mr. SMITH, jun.,
Ironmonger—Mr. BELLAMY—Mr. DALES, Grocer—Mr. PARKER, Stationer—
Mr. HOBSON—Mr. WATMOUGH, Baker—CAPT. WATERLAND—of Mr. PEARSON,
Grimsby Toll-gate—and at the CHAPELS and PREACHING HOUSES throughout
the Grimsby Circuit. Early application for Tickets is requested.

☞ *A Collection at the close of each Service in behalf of the Building Fund.*

Skelton, Printer, Grimsby

LEFT: Opening services of the new Wesleyan chapel, Grimsby, 1847.
RIGHT: Early Class Tickets. OPPOSITE ABOVE: Wesleyan Prayer
Leaders' Plan for Louth, 1846. BELOW: Wesleyan chapel in Eastgate,
Louth, enlarged in 1820 to have the three entrances; above the old
Wesleyan Sunday School in Lee Street. (DNR) INSET: John Hannah,
President of the Conference 1842 and 1851.

THE
WESLEYAN PRAYER-LEADERS' PLAN,

"Pray without ceasing."
1 Thess. v. 17.

FOR LOUTH AND ADJACENT VILLAGES, 1846.

"Be not weary in well-doing."
2 Thess. iii. 13.

PLACES. Sunday Evening.	Hour.	J. 25	FEBRUARY. 1	8	15	22	MARCH. 1	8	15	22	29	APRIL. 5	12	19	26
CHAPEL OR VESTRY	Eight.	1	10	15		16	3	11	5	12	6		15	9	16
BUNTING LANE	—	3	8	16		15	4	12	7	13	14		16	12	15
KILN YARD, Donner's	—	15	12	2	Sacrament.	1	5	16	8	14	13	Sacrament.	9	15	3
SPITAL HILL	—	16	7	9		14	6	15	10	2	5		1	16	8
BURWELL	Six.		5	1			7		9		3		4		2
FARFORD	—		14	5			8		6		10		11		7
RAITHBY	—		6	3			9		1		11		2		10
STEWTON	—		2	4			10		2		12		6		13
SOUTH ELKINGTON	—		11	6			12		4		7		5		14
MANBY	—	9	3	13			2		8		4		14		

THURSDAY EVENING.

		J. 29	FEBRUARY. 5	12	19	26	MARCH. 5	12	19	26	APRIL. 2	9	16	23	30
RIVER HEAD	½ past 7	15	16	13	8	5	4	3	2	1	15	16	5	13	14

Names of the Prayer Leaders.

1. Shepherd, Rogerson, Mackinder, Kime, S. Brown.
2. Hoyle, Slight, Desforges, W. Cash.
3. Boothby, Hall, J. Pearson, Raspin.
4. W. Ashton, W. Shepherd, Garnett, Bains.
5. W. Pearson, 1st, Goodwin, Odlin, Easting.
6. Jacklin, Furnish, Bingham, Squire, Colam.
7. Boswell, Thompson, 1st, Dowse, Sutton.
8. H. Pearson, Sanderson, Brown, Borrill.
9. J. Ashton, Snowdon, Smith, C. Oates.
10. Mason, Hall, Youle, Askey.
11. Gelsthorpe, Pearson, 2nd, G. Rushforth, T. Oates.
12. England, Cook, Bennett, Thompson, 2nd.
13. Ingamells, Burt, Hatcliffe, Hill.
14. Broughton, Wright, Wakelin, M. Harrison.
15. Crampton, Longbottom, White, Youle, Mason, Maddison, Beech.
16. Topham, Scholey, Atkinson, Bywaters, Tomlinson, Robinson.

N.B. Every Prayer Leader must attend to his own appointment, or get his place supplied by one whose name is on the plan.

A Meeting of the Prayer Leaders will be held on Wednesday Evening, April 1st, at which all are desired to attend.

W. Shepherd, Printer, Market-Place, Louth.

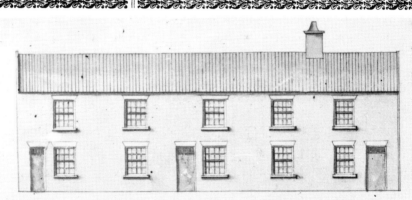

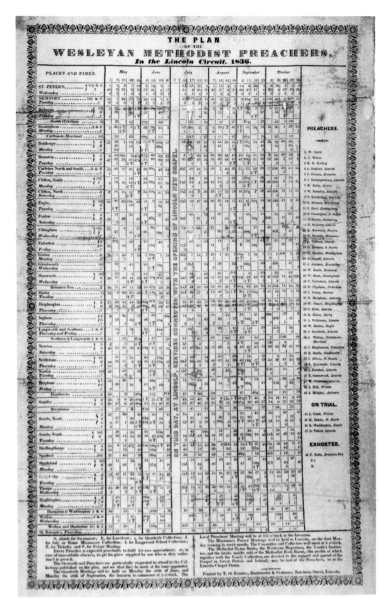

Wesleyan Preachers' Plan, Lincoln, showing opening of Wesley chapel on 2 July 1836.

ABOVE: Rosemary Lane Wesleyan day school, Lincoln. BELOW: Kelstern Hall, in the Wolds near Louth, home of the Sharpleys.

Paul Rigall (1750-1836), and his wife Mary (1753-1839), two ardent early Methodists. (Both DNR)

Sunday School attendance card for Louth, 1829.

This is to certify that

John Saunderson

has attended the *Methodist Sunday School*, in Louth, fifteen Sundays, being neither late nor absent, and is thereby entitled to the esteem of the *Managers*.

Fifteenth year 1829

HYMNS

TO BE SUNG BY THE CHILDREN

OF THE

WESLEYAN SUNDAY SCHOOL,

MARKET RASEN,

Sunday, September 11th, 1864.

HYMN I.

THE Bible! the Bible! more precious than gold,
The hopes and the glories its pages unfold;
It speaks of a Saviour, and tells of his love;
It shows us the way to the mansions above.

The Bible! the Bible! blest volume of truth,
How sweetly it smiles on the season of youth;
It bids us seek early the pearl of great price,
Ere the heart is enslaved in the bondage of vice.

The Bible! the Bible! we hail it with joy,
Its truths and its glories our tongues shall employ;
We'll sing of its triumphs, we'll tell of its worth,
And send its glad tidings afar o'er the earth

The Bible! the Bible! the valleys shall ring,
And hill-tops re-echo the notes that we sing;
Our banners inscribed with its precepts and rules,
Shall long wave in triumph, the joy of our schools.

HYMN II.

JOYFULLY, joyfully, onward we move,
Bound to the land of bright spirits above;
Jesus, our Saviour, in mercy says " Come!"
Joyfully, joyfully, haste to your home.
Soon will our pilgrimage end here below,
Soon to the presence of God we shall go;
Then, if to Jesus our hearts have been given,
Joyfully, joyfully, rest we in heaven.

Teachers and scholars have passed on before,
Waiting, they watch us approaching the shore,
Singing to cheer us, while passing along,
"Joyfully, joyfully, haste to your home!"
Songs of sweet music there ravish the ear,
Harps of the blessed, your strains we shall hear,
Filling with harmony heaven's high dome;
Joyfully, joyfully, Jesus, we come!

Death with his arrow may soon lay us low,
Safe in our Saviour, we fear not the blow;
Jesus hath broken the bars of the tomb,
Joyfully, joyfully, we will go home!
Bright will the morn of eternity dawn,
Death will be conquer'd, his sceptre be gone:
Over the plains of sweet Canaan we'll roam,
Joyfully, joyfully, safely at home!

HYMN III.

Hark! the joyous sound is swelling,
   Hark! the song of Jubilee;
Of the Saviour's triumphs telling,
   Of His conquests yet to be;
     Jubilate! Jubilate!
Christ shall reign from sea to sea.

See the Gospel banner waving
   Where the Hindoo's temple stood;
See the Isles of Fiji craving
   For the bread of life as food;
     Jubilate! Jubilate!
They no longer thirst for blood.

Far and near our churches flourish,
   Myriads chant their joyful lays,
Schools, the children guide and nourish,
   Old and young Hosannas raise;
     Jubilate! Jubilate!
Great Redeemer, Thee they praise.

Wider fields are still before us
   Where to sow the precious seed;
And that seed from heaven's rich storehouse
   Will supply the world's vast need;
     Jubilate! Jubilate!
Onward let the work proceed.

Bring your offerings, Christians, bring them,
   Bring your offerings rich and poor;
Bring your sons and daughters, bring them—
   Let them enter every door;
     Jubilate! Jubilate!
Spread the tidings more and more.

R. HACKETT, PRINTER QUEEN STREET, MARKET RASEN.

Hymns for the Wesleyan Sunday School, Market Rasen, 1864.

They Started Young

Important as were the buildings, the real strength and the annual growth of Methodism was in the people. In March 1761 Wesley was in Leeds and convened a meeting of all his preachers. After consultation he wrote: 'I find the work of God increases on every side, but particularly in Lincolnshire, where there has been no work like this since the time I preached on my father's tomb'. That was early comment, and might equally have been said fifty years afterwards, for the statistics alone reveal a tremendous surge forward, which was to be the pattern well into the 19th century.

The circuit system, which became a characteristic of Methodism, was hardly recognised in the early days. Lincolnshire was known as East and West at first, the east stretching from the Humber to the Welland, and the west from the Ouse to Grantham and spilling over into Nottinghamshire and Yorkshire. The Methodists lived on a large map, but that was too large. The division of circuits enabled the preachers as well as the people to concentrate their gifts in a limited and defined area. Soon the circuits were to be known and localised — Epworth, Grimsby, Louth, Horncastle, Gainsborough, Lincoln, Spalding, Barton on Humber — all these before the end of the 18th century, and other divisions followed as the population grew and as the Methodist family enlarged.

Two things contributed to the increase in membership and influence: the enlargement of the local society and the setting up of new societies. The two were complementary and interwoven. It was the missionary zeal of ordinary people which gave impetus to the local work, and the same zeal led them to pioneer causes beyond the confines of their own homes. In addition to this local effort, there were periods of what is called 'revival'.

James Barry, the Superintendent at Epworth in 1781, said that some of his brethren had for several years 'been crying to God to revive his work in this remarkably dead place. Three months ago there seemed to be some answer'. Nightly prayer meetings were held in Epworth and, after six weeks, the society increased by eighty members. The revival continued into the next year. Meetings were held in several homes and people were being converted.

Associated with the same revival, Thomas Saxton reported: 'We have in Epworth three factories for spinning yarn and weaving coarse linen cloth; the children employed here, both boys and girls, were the most profligate in the town. It was nine or ten days after this, that some of the girls of the largest factory, sent and desired me to come to them; but I did not go. Then they went to Ann Towris and Ann Field, who went to them many times, and spared no pains in talking to them . . . After a while I went to the factory myself, and saw the fruit of their labours'. Saxton may have been timid at facing a bevy of profligate girls at the factory, but he was keen to inform Wesley of what had been done and Wesley himself visited the factory. 'The whole scene was changed', he wrote in his Journal. 'In three of the factories no more lewdness or profaneness were found; for God had put a new song in their mouth, and blasphemies were turned to praise'.

41

In 1791 a similar revival took place in Grimsby and Cleethorpes, and it was that intrepid Meggie, Amos Appleyard who, by his prayers and his exhortations, stirred the people. The twenty-six members at Cleethorpes increased to fifty-four and in Grimsby the increase was the same.

Sporadic revivals of this kind gave a boost to a society. One of the converts at Epworth was Alexander Kilham, a name we shall meet again, who joined Wesley's itinerants. But in other parts of the county significant results had far-reaching effects. George Shadford, a native of Scotter, spent his early life in the army. He says: 'When our company lay in quarters at Gainsborough, I went with a sergeant to the place where the Methodists frequently preached, which was the old hall . . . We did not go with the design of getting any good for our souls; but to meet two young women . . . in order to walk with them in the afternoon'. The preacher's word struck deep in the heart of Shadford: 'I thought no more about the girls whom I went to meet; and found that I had work enough to take care of my own soul. I now went every Sunday when there was preaching'.

Shadford went home to tell his parents of the good news and told it so convincingly that they too became members of the Scotter society. When his army career ended, he joined the ranks of Wesley's preachers, and soon was off to America. As he embarked for this work he had in his pocket a letter from Wesley: 'I let you loose, George, on that great continent of America. Publish your message in the open face of the sun, and do all the good you can'.

Richard Watson was born at Barton upon Humber and, with his parents moved to Lincoln when he was eight years old. He was a rebel to religion, but loved learning, was a capable mathematician and, when he came into contact with a watchmaker, who was a Methodist, he was encouraged to attend the Waterside chapel and was there converted. On the day following his fifteenth birthday he preached his first sermon in John Mayfield's kitchen at Boothby. He was soon in the ministry, became a leading theologian, founded the Methodist Missionary Society and rose to the rank of President.

Frederick James Jobson came to Lincoln in early childhood, attended a class meeting whilst still a boy, listened to outdoor preaching in front of his father's house and was converted under the evangelical zeal of John Smith, a Lincoln minister. Smith was in the city only two years, but hundreds of people came under his influence. One such was John Hunt, another youth, born at Hykeham Moor, who became a farm labourer at Swinderby and was converted under John Smith at Thorpe on the Hill. 'I cried aloud for mercy', he says, 'for the sake of Christ, while I was in a minute as completely bathed in tears and perspiration as if I had been thrown into a river'.

Both Jobson and Hunt were born in the same year, 1812, were together in the Lincoln Methodist society, but soon their ways parted. For Jobson it was the ministry at City Road, London and other provincial cities, Book Steward and President; for Hunt it was a Missionary to Fiji and in ten successful years he completed his course. His memorial is in the 1909 chapel at Thorpe on the Hill, with relics of his Fijian life in the Museum of Lincolnshire Life.

They had another friend in the notorious Thomas Cooper; he joined the Lincoln society under the leadership of Edward Shipham, a 'man of no more than ordinary powers of mind', who inspired Cooper to become a preacher. It was a short-lived experience, however, for within six years Cooper ceased his links with Methodism and devoted his energies and affections to other things.

When Methodist societies had truly established themselves in either an improvised building or some more permanent chapel, and when the itinerant system was consolidated and a preaching plan introduced, the activities of local people centred in Sunday worship and weeknight classes. But there was also early concern for the children. Rex Russell of Hull University has researched Sunday Schools in Lindsey, calling them 'a miserable compromise' — a compromise between finding money for adequate teaching in formal educational establishments, and using voluntary help in a system which allowed only one day a week, Sunday, the only day when work ceased. In addition to the voluntary help and the only free day to exercise it, was the already existing building — the chapel. Sunday schools were therefore the forerunners of the day school, and the church, both Anglican and nonconformist, provided amenities in both material and staff, trained or otherwise. Russell concludes that for children of 'the labouring poor' Sunday schools were very important.

How much was done before 1800 is difficult to determine. The first Sunday school in Lincoln began in 1806 in a room hired by John Hannah. It was situated on the Waterside and it seems that Hannah, only fourteen years of age, was both prime mover and the first teacher. A second school was built uphill and a third in Down Street. 'About 300 children have been regularly taught the principles of Christianity from sabbath to sabbath throughout the year in these schools, and to the superior scholars writing is also taught during the evening in the week'. This report comes from Abraham Watmough, a Minister in Lincoln in 1828. He reported similar work in North Scarle.

A school was started in Grimsby in 1808 by Joseph Plaskett, but it had little success until Thomas Winteringham joined the society; then it prospered. There were soon several centres and with every new chapel erected there was provision for a school. By 1823 there were 198 pupils taught by upwards of seventy teachers. An annual report for that year stated the objects of the teachers and also appealed for funds. They aimed at 'teaching the rising generation, the first principles of the Christian religion, and to revere the sacred pages of Revelation'. The income to cover the expense of running the school was derived, for the most part, from an annual collection taken at the chapel.

The next year the income doubled, mainly by subscriptions. And who could resist the appeal when the committee declared that their aim was to give Religious Education: 'A Property, of which no adverse circumstances can deprive them — a fortune which the hand of dishonesty cannot pilfer — a plant which the pestiferous breath of malice cannot blight, a flower which the gelid grasp of poverty cannot blast — a treasure which the hand of time cannot corrode — a jewel, the lustre of which the filth of scandal cannot tarnish — a gem which increases its value, and shines with greater brilliancy, when the clouds of adversity settle on its hand'.

At Binbrook a school was opened in 1819 with 100 scholars and 28 teachers. Market Rasen began even earlier, when upwards of ninety children were admitted. Many Sunday schools were opened with a view to their being interdenominational, although they were under the wing of either church or chapel people. In Kirton Lindsey a schoolroom was built with the notice over the doorway: 'Wesleyan schoolroom for children of all denominations 1827'. Laceby declared clearly that their first school was for all children of all denominations.

The establishment of the Sunday school led soon to the creation of the Sunday School Anniversary and field days, the object of both to extend the appeal for funds and to provide a kind of shop window to the public at large. At Nettleham 'the teachers and children assembled at 9 o'clock in the morning and walked in procession round the village and its vicinity, accompanied with music and singing, the teachers soliciting contributions for the ensuing years'. At Barton upon Humber Easter Monday was the great day when they 'paraded the town, accompanied by their teachers, when their clean and neat appearance, and the pretty style in which they sang, occasioned general admiration'. The anniversaries also gave the children an opportunity to display their latent gifts by singing and recitations.

Libraries were established in all the schools. Most had their own written rules. The Cleethorpes Wesleyan Library declared that its aim was to 'supply the mental wants of an increasing and better instructed population; to afford amusing and useful occupation to the hours of relaxation from business . . . making them wiser, better, and more useful members of civil, social, and religious society'. The rules ran to about a dozen clauses, defining times of opening and general discipline. By the middle of the 19th century there were over 300 Sunday schools attached to the chapels with nearly 24,000 scholars, being taught by some 6,000 teachers, all of whom were unpaid.

All this points to the increasing success of the schools in the Victorian period, and these led to the establishment of the future Wesleyan Day Schools. All the day schools sprang from the initiative of the leading personnel in the chapels, not only in Lincoln city, which set up its famous Rosemary Lane day school, but in a large number of towns and villages. All these served their generation and only changed character and ethos with the changing educational requirements of the 1870 and 1902 Education Acts.

OPPOSITE LEFT: Opening of Victoria chapel, Grimsby, 1860. RIGHT: Circuit Steward Mr J. Gibson was also a Trustee of 15 chapels in the Sleaford Circuit. ABOVE: John Hunt, who entered the Ministry 1838, was a missionary to Fiji, and died 1848. (DNR) CENTRE: Wesleyan Foreign Missions at Humberston, 1862. BELOW: Rev John Smith.

Wesleyan
FOREIGN MISSIONS.
On Sunday, February 9th, 1862,
TWO SERMONS
WILL BE PREACHED
In the Wesleyan Chapel, Humberston,
BY
THE REV. WILLIAM WILSON,
RETURNED MISSIONARY FROM FIJI,
Service to commence at Two and Six p.m.

On Monday, February the 10th,
A SERMON WILL BE PREACHED IN THE SAME PLACE BY
The Rev. Gervase Smith,
OF MANCHESTER,
Service to commence at half-past Two, p.m.
IN THE EVENING OF THE SAME DAY THE
ANNUAL MEETING
WILL BE HELD, AND
Addressed by the REVS. GERVASE SMITH, W. WILSON,
and other MINISTERS.
Joseph Bennett, Esq., will preside.
Service to commence at 6½ p.m.
A Collection at each Service in aid of the above Missions.

45

GRIMSBY CIRCUIT, 1837.

Price 3d.

WESLEYAN PREACHERS' PLAN.

PLACES.	TIME	AUG 6	13	20	27	SEP 3	10	17	24	OCT 1	8	15	22	29
Grimsby	10½	3	4	16	2	13	1	19	4	3	2	9	1	22
	2	30	4	1s	2	4q	1	2	4	1	2L	4	1k	2s
	6	30	4	1	2	4q	1	2	4	1	2	4	1k	2
Caistor	2-6	17	2	4	1s	2q	4	1	2	30	1k	2	4	1
Cleethorps	9	9		1		4		2q		1s		4		2k
	6	13	15	16	17	18	12	19q	28	20	29	9	30	22k
Laceby	9		2		1		4		2		1		4	
	2	8		9L		16q		13		11		3k		18
	6	4	24	2	29	1q	22	4	30	2s	8	1k	17	4
Tetney	10		30		32		9		36		17		25	
	2	29		19		11q		10		12		13		28
	6	29	25	19	4	11q	18	10	1s	12	34	27	2k	28
Humberstone	10	29		19		11		10		34		13		28
	2		30		4		9q		1		17k		2s	
	6		30		32		9q		12		17k		15	
Thoresby	2	20		15		25		22		4		32k		12
	6		29		30q		34		9		10		11	
Holton	10		1		8		2s		10		4		12	
	6	20	18	27	19	25	30q	22	34	4	15	32k	35	29
Waltham	2		1		8q		2		10		4k		12	
	6	19	1	20	18q	22	2s	24	25	29	4k	30	9	11
Scartho	9		12		4		25q		32		29		30k	
	6	32	22	3	34	15	11q	36	27	28	12	16	21k	20
Hatcliffe	2		32		18q		17		8		31		18	
	6	24		26		27		9		15k		24		10
Barnoldby	2	19		20		22q		24		29		30		11k
	6		32		27		17		8		31		18	
Ashby	2		29		30q		34		9		10		11	
	6	27		10		19		20		18		22k		35
Limber	10	17		4		2q		1		2k		2		1s
	2		11		26		20		33		24		32	
Keelby	2	4	20	2	9q	1	8	4	13	2s	11	1k	19	4
Stallingbro'	2	18	19	17	21	20q	29	33	24	22	30k	8	28	9
Great Coates	2		9		11		13q		16		19		3k	
Little Coates	10½	22		28		16		13		11		21		18
Bradley	2	21		3		25q		32		9		13k	
Brigsley	6	34		35		19q		29		20		10k	
Wold Newton	1½	34		35		19		29		20		10	
Ravendale	2	27		8		19		20		18		22		36
Irby	2	24		29		22q		30		8		17k	
Thorganby	2	24		26		27		9		15		24		10
Nettleton	6	26		24		23q		31		7		26		33k
Rothwell	6		23		24		26		31		33		23	
Cabourne	6	33		23		24		26		31		23		7

Preachers. Residence.

1 JONES, ... Grimsby.
2 HOCKEN, ...Grimsby.
3 Hopewell, ... Grimsby.
4 Walker, ...Grimsby.
5 Cunningham,... Scartho.
6 Marris, ... Stallingbro'.
7 Saunby, ...Caistor.
8 Hewson, ... Barnoldby.
9 T. Bellamy, ...Grimsby.
10 J. Temple, ... Waithe.
11 W. Temple, ... Waltham.
12 Blow, ... Humberstone.
13 J. Bellamy, ...Grimsby.
14 Taylor, ... Stallingbro.'
15 Forman, ...Waltham.
16 Poxon, ... Grimsby.
17 Brown, ...Grimsby.
18 Turner, ... Holton.
19 Smethurst, ...Grimsby.
20 Read, ... Grimsby.
21 Askey, ...Great Coates.
22 G. Marris, ... Grimsby.
23 Lingard, ...Caistor.
24 Wigglesworth,.. Caistor.
25 Miller, ... Tetney.
26 Smith, ...Caistor.
27 Davidson, ... Ashby.
28 Leesing, ...Cleethorps.
29 Wilson,... ... Holton.
30 Carter, ...Scartho.
31 Rhodes,... ... Caistor.

ON TRIAL.

32 Mells, ...Grimsby.
33 Twigg, ... Limber.
34 Howden, ...Tetney.

EXHORTERS.

35 M.————36 R.

References.

L Lovefeast.
S Sacrament.
q Quarterly Collection.
k Kingswood Collection.

Missionary Anniversaries will be held at Cleethorpes, Aug. 21st; Holton, Aug. 22nd; Scartho, Oct. 10; Limber, Oct 11; Stallingbro', Oct. 12; Hatcliffe, Oct. 16; and Barnoldby, Oct. 17.

Quarterly Meeting will be held at Grimsby, on Monday Oct. 2nd. The Stewards are to meet precisely at 3 o'clock, and the Local Preachers at ½ past 6, who will take tea with the Stewards at ½ past 5 o'clock

N.B. Every Preacher is expected to attend to his appointments, or provide a proper substitute.

(Skelton, Printer, Grimsby.) (Price 1½d.)

Grimsby Circuit Wesleyan Preachers' Plan, 1837.

PLAN OF THE APPOINTMENTS,
OF THE WESLEYAN METHODIST PREACHERS,
For the Town of LOUTH,
During the re-building of the Chapel: 1835.

REFERENCES.

S. Stands for the Lord's Supper : B. Baptism : m. Society Meeting: L. Love Feast: Q. Quarterly Collection in aid of the Circuit : k. Collection for Kingswood & Woodhouse Grove Schools.

PLACES AND HOURS.

		SEPTEMBER.				OCTOBER.				NOVEMBER.		
		6	13	20	27	4	11	18	25	1	8	15	22
		II. Kings 10. Matt. 7	II. Kings 19 Matt.14	Jer. 5 Matt. 21	Jer. 35 Matt. 28	Ezek. 2 Mark 7	Ezek. 14 Mark 14	Ezek 20 Luke 4	Dan. 3 Luke 11	Joel 2 Heb. 12	Hab. 2 Luke 24	Prov. 2 John 7	Prov. 11 John 14
GUILD-HALL, {10½		6	1	22Q	3	1	2	3	1B	2	3k	1	2
	6	3	1	2Q	3	1	2	3	1M	2	3k	1	2
INDEPENDENT CHAPEL,	2	3	27	2Q	3	1	L	3s	1	2	3k	8	10
DITTO, *Wednesday Evening,*	7	3	1	2	3	1	2	3	1	2	3	1	2
SUNDAY SCHOOL, *Lee Street* {10½		23	40	41Q	5	13	6	8	9	27	22k	5	26
	6	27	21	32Q	42	44	14	17	23	7	16k	35	40
W. PEARSON'S, *Eastgate,*	6	25	8	9Q	24	16	26	40	32	24	41k	14	6
RIVER-HEAD,	6	17	5	7Q	8	45	25	42	35	43	37k	44	24

PREACHERS' NAMES.

1 W. HORTON,	14 M. PLASKITT,	32 J. PORTER,
2 C. HAYDON,	16 W. MAWER,	35 F. WHITAKER,
3 S. DIXON,	17 T. SMITH,	37 J. HUBBARD,
5 M. BURMAN,	21 J. B. SHARPLEY,	40 J. M'DOWELL,
6 J. BENNETT,	22 JESSE SHARPLEY,	41 F. RIGGALL,
7 G. EASTING,	23 T. TOPHAM,	42 T. CHATTERTON,
8 J. STEPHENSON,	24 J. HOBSON,	43 J. BRETT,
9 J. HUNT,	25 T. SHAW,	44 G. PEARSON,
10 J. LARDER.	26 W. BURKITT,	45 J. LILL.
13 H. R. ALLENBY,	27 E. RYALL,	

[T. Smith, Printer, Louth.]

Special Plan for Louth during re-building. 1835.

State.	Ludborough Class Month. Meets on Sun Days.	Station.	October 1820				November 1820				December				Q. D.	Yearly Sub.
			8	15	22	30	5	12	19	26	3	10	17	24	31	
	Cornelius Foster Leader	m	a	p	p	p	p	p	p	p	p	p	p	p	5.0	
	Eleanor Foster	m	a	p	p	p	p	p	p	p	p	p	a	p	2.6	
	William Stamp	w	a	p	a	p	p	p	p	p	p	p	a	a	~	
	John Pearson	m	p	p	a	p	p	p	a	p	p	a	p	p	1~	
	John East	m	a	p	a	a	a	p	a	p	a	s	s	h	a	1~
	Dinah East	m	a	s	a	a	a	p	p	s	p	p	s	a	~	
	George Swaby		p	p	p	p		p	p	p	a	p	p	1~	
	Ruth White	w	a	a	a	p	p	a	a	a	a	a	a	a	1~	
	Mary Broadley	m	a				a	p	a	p	p	a	a	p	~6	
	Mary Wilson	s	p				p	p	p	p	p	p	p	1~	
	Susannah Watson		a	p	a	p	a	p	a	p	a	a	a	D.6	
	Ann Pearson	m	p	p	a	p	a	a	a	a	p	a	p	a	1~	
	Reb.ª Clarke	m	p	p	a	p	a	p	p	p	p	a	p	h	~	
	Thomas Watson	m	a	p	a	a	p	p	a	p	a	a	p	a	~6	
	William Throop	m	p	p	p	p	p	p	p	p	p	p	p	5~	
	Mary Throop	m	p	p	a	p	p	p	a	p	p	a	p	p	~	
	Sarah Lill	m	a	p	a	p	a	p	a	p	a	p	a	a	~6	
	Frances Riggall	s	p	p	a	p	p	a	a	p	a	p	a	a	~6	
	Mary Rawson	s													~6	
	Month		January				February				March			(1821)		
	Meets on Sundays		7	14	21	28	4	11	18	25	4	11	18	25	1	
1	Cornelius Foster	m	p	p	p	p	p	p	p	p	p	p	p	p	5.0	
2	Eleanor Do	m	p	p	p	p	p	p	p	p	p	p	p	p		
3	William Stamp	w	p	p	p	p	p	p	p	p	a	p	p	a	~1~	
4	John Pearson	m	p	p	p	p	p	p	a	p	a	p	p	a	1~	
5	John East	m	p	a	a	a	p	a	p	a	p	a	p	p		
6	Dinah Do	m	p	p	p	p	p	p	p	p	a	s	a	a		
7	George Swaby	o	p	p	p	p	p	p	p	p	a	p	p	p	1~0	
8	Ruth White	w	a	p	a	p	p	s	s	o	s	s	s	s	1~0	
9	Mary Broadley	m	a			a	p	a	p	a	a	a	p	p		
10	Mary Wilson	o	a	p		a	p	p	p	p	p	p	p	a		
11	Susanah Watson	m	p	a	o		p	p	D	a	p	a	D	p		
12	Ann Pearson	m	a	p	a	p	a	p	a	p	a	a	p	a		
13	Reb.ª Clark	m	p	p	p	a	p	p	a	p	a	p	p	p		
14	Thomas Watson	m	a	a	p	s	p	a	p	a	a	s	a		
15	William Throop	m	p	p	p	p	a	p	p	p	p	p	a	p		
16	Mary Do	m	p	p	a	p	p	p	p	p	p	p	p	p		
17	Sarah Lill	m	a	p	a	p	a	a	a	p	a	p	a	a	~6	
18	Francis Riggale	o	a	p	p	p	p	a	a	p	a	p	a	a	~6	1~0
	Mary Rawson	o	p													

N. B.—Every Leader is requested to mark his Class-paper as follows:—In the column under Station, for single Person, put S; a married ditto, M; a Widow or Widower, W.—In the column under State, a expresses awakened—á, deeply convinced of sin—(?) one whose state is dubious—(.) one who is just fled—(○) one professing full redemption—The Quarterly Fasts are, the first Friday after New Year's Day, after Lady Day, after Midsummer Day, and after Michaelmas Day.

Hand-written Class List for Ludborough, 1820.

48

ABOVE: Old Wesleyan chapel, Willingham by Stow, 1811. BELOW: The enlarged Louth Wesleyan chapel, 1835. (DNR)

ABOVE: Thatched cottage at Haven Bank in Wildmore Fen, where services were held before the chapel was built. (HL) BELOW: Interior of Theddlethorpe Wesleyan chapel.

The Ranters

It is only partly true to say that Primitive Methodism had in origin similar features to the work of Wesley and his preachers. Both movements, it is true, began outdoors; both formed societies; both built numerous chapels, in the early days much alike in appearance; both established the circuit system, and both were eventually constituted into a Connexion.

The point where likenesses end was in the type of person who originated the movements and the type of person attracted by them. Hugh Bourne and William Clowes, the chief leaders in the Primitive Methodist revival, did not possess the background which Wesley brought to his work; they had not the same ability and temperament, but they did possess an experience of conversion which was translated into a deep concern for their fellow men. Like Wesley, these two broke with tradition, but never did they seek to return to the Wesleyan body which had dismembered them. They became the architects of a new type of Methodism.

Primitive Methodism was not entirely a break with Wesleyanism, rather it was a new spirit of revival, charismatic in emphasis, and distinguished from the Wesley revival in that Bourne and Clowes adopted an American brand of evangelism, most notably in what became known as Camp Meetings. These were ill-timed in some respects, owing to the troubles in the industrial life of the country (1807-10). The Wesleyan Conference declared them to be 'highly improper, and likely to be productive of considerable mischief. And we disclaim all connection with them'.

The movement in Lincolnshire originated from missioning activity in Nottinghamshire. It entered the county in the south at Grantham, and in the north at Gainsborough. They were almost simultaneous and by different agents. It spread more speedily in the north than in the south, largely because Lindsey was more thickly populated, while the more conservative south, less populated, was also dominated by a strong Catholic tradition.

The two most prominent names were John Wedgwood and William Braithwaite. Wedgwood was one of the famous Staffordshire potters, who inherited the business, only to give it all up when he became converted under Primitive Methodist preaching in 1809. He himself became a preacher and was soon standing at the market cross in Grantham, where he was arrested and put in prison. The crowd who attended followed him to the Guildhall, singing as they moved along the street. Wedgwood was tried and committed to the Quarter Sessions. William Lockwood, hearing of the arrest, hastened from Staffordshire to Grantham. He too preached at the market cross and, like Wedgwood, was arrested, but saved himself from imprisonment by promising to return home forthwith.

The news of Wedgwood's arrest reached Tunstall, the headquarters of the movement, where Thomas Woodnorth, a gifted poet, turned the event into some 170 lines of heroic verse, but that did not help Wedgwood in his cell. William Clowes took a more practical line and hurried off to the scene, or as near to the scene as he thought fit. He called on Lockwood at East Bridgford, only to hear that Wedgwood was free, having entered into his own recognizances and was in Buckminster preaching once more.

A glimpse of Wedgwood in prison affords a sidelight on how Primitive Methodist preachers faced that kind of situation, for Wedgwood was not the only preacher to be jailed for outdoor preaching. Whilst in prison he was befriended by a youth named Sammy Bailey. Sarah Kirkland visited him and found him 'happy in God'. He too wrote some verse to pass the time and not unnaturally recalled his arrest:

'At Grantham cross I did appear,
The constable did then draw near;
And from the cross they laid me down,
But could not take away my crown.'

The second attempt to establish Primitive Methodism in Lincolnshire was as strange as it was different. A camp meeting was attended by Sir William Manners. His presence there, to say the least, was unusual, for he was no champion of the Primitive Methodists, but was there to serve his own ends. His purpose was to collect John Benton, the preacher, and bring him back to Grantham. Benton rather enjoyed the ride, for it gave him an unexpected opportunity of explaining to Sir William the 'plan of salvation', which, in the course of the journey, he did with no little pride. On arrival in Grantham Sir William took him to the stone pulpit which he had prepared on his own ground near the Guildhall and Benton was ushered in to it and given freedom of speech.

It was all a plot on the part of Sir William Manners to show the town burgesses that the parliamentary candidate whom they had rejected was the very man Sir William had supported. Whatever the effect upon the town burgesses, it gave Sir William a secure place in Thomas Woodnorth's verse:

'Lo, Grantham's famous pulpit made of stone;
Frought with good zeal, witness Sir William's hand,
The Knight of Buckminster, who made a stand
Against the sons of envy in the fight . . . '

Neither Benson's exhortation from the stone pulpit, nor Wedgwood's preaching at the market cross, resulted in the establishment of a Primitive Methodist society in Grantham, and more than a dozen years passed before any attempt was made again.

Meanwhile in Gainsborough, William Braithwaite and Thomas Saxton opened their commission by singing in the streets as they walked to the market place. Thomas Cooper, noticed earlier, was a lad of fourteen and he turned aside to see what was going on. 'They were called Ranters by the crowd,' he said, 'but I soon learned that they termed themselves Primitive Methodists.' From this inauspicious beginning the 'Ranters' took the small chapel in Church Lane which Wesley once used, and Cooper, along with about a dozen youths, joined the infant society.

William Braithwaite was an effective evangelist and much in earnest in both praying and preaching. His stay in the county was long enough for him to be dubbed 'The Apostle of north-west Lincolnshire'. When he took his stand at the village cross in Appleby and began as usual by singing, a steward of the estate ordered him to stop, but he defied the order as the crowd increased, and was dislodged from his stand. The outcome of his preaching was the formation of a society in the house of Robert Keightley. Braithwaite was the first preacher in Messingham and among his hearers was Thomas Kendall, whose six sons all became Ministers. One sequel of the preaching was that Thomas Kendall opened his own house for services at Ashby.

So effective was Braithwaite in the village of Wildsworth that he gathered most of the local farmers in support of the cause and they erected a little chapel on the banks of the Trent. George Smith of Bishop Norton, a Wesleyan preacher, had been praying for revival in his own village, and his prayers were answered when Braithwaite came. The preaching led to the formation of a class, the opening of Smith's house for services, and soon the building of a chapel, all within the space of two years. Another Wesleyan was William Bellham, a class leader and preacher but, feeling the need for revival within himself as well as among his people, he came into contact with Braithwaite, joined the Primitive Methodists and joyfully declared that he had never seen 'so much of God in a man before; he was all love'.

With the successes of William Braithwaite, Hugh Bourne sent Thomas King into Lincolnshire. He entered the 'out-of the world' county in August 1819, starting at Market Rasen, where already Ann Carr had attempted some open-air preaching, and where John Harrison, a freelance preacher had set up a small society. King moved over the 'moors, wolds, clays and marshes' to Grimsby, 'the most dreary of all watering places'. He was the first Primitive Methodist in the town and commenced his preaching on waste ground in Victoria Street, delivering his sermon from a wheelbarrow. This unspectacular start proved effective, and on the same night William Holt, a farmer from Clee, invited King to his home. The Grimsby society dates from this time, and soon a disused chapel became available in Loft Street and from there the society grew.

Thomas King was joined by George Herod and 'numbers are added to our society daily'. At North Thoresby 'our people have only visited it about six months, and now we have in society eighty members, most of whom have been noted for wickedness'. King moved to Louth and in the villages around there was a great awakening: 'the devil was forced to fly and sinners cried out for mercy'.

Across the county Francis Birch was preaching in Alford, set up a class in the house of John Green, and then went to Boston and from there the revival spread across the fens. There is something modest and pitifully incomplete in Birch's diary, but one detects an earnestness in what he was doing. 'The Lord was powerfully present and precious to many souls'. At Fishtoft he 'felt his soul much alive to God and growing zeal for his glory, and the salvation of precious souls'.

There was opposition in many places. When John Hallsworth preached for the first time in Lincoln he was in mortal danger of his life. 'Mobs were raised up at almost every place. Eggs were flying together with stones and dirt: cocks were fighting, bells were ringing, men were drinking and smoking, and holding up their hats and hollooing . . . ' William Fieldsend was treated similarly at Welbourne and Waddington, 'but we came out of the fire unhurt'.

William Clowes came to Lincoln and, reflecting upon his adventures, set down the record of his visit in dramatic prose: 'We began the labours of the day about nine in the morning and terminated them at about nine at night. About eleven o'clock in the forenoon, the conflict with the powers of darkness was very hot. A goat which some sons of Belial procured, was run in among the congregation with a shout of three times three, and throwing dust in the air. But we remained on firm phalanx amid the storm, and returned upon the legion of the devil a powerful discharge from the big guns of Sinai, whilst at the same time we unfurled the ensigns of the cross of Jesus, inviting the enemy to ground arms, and surrender upon the terms of peace and reconciliation offered in the gospel'.

One gets the impression that Clowes rather enjoyed the day. His holy war resulted in the formation of a society which soon rented a room in Mint Lane, and the work spread all around the city. Says William Wilbur: 'I laboured with sister Perry in this part for six months and the Lord raised up many societies'.

In Fulbeck a preacher from Leadenham, when preaching in the open air, was arrested by the constable, who was so impressed by what he heard, that he joined the Methodists himself. George Jenkinson tells of seven years of preaching in Fulbeck, 'where, indoors and outdoors, they were assailed with opposition'. John Hallsworth says 'a gun was brought and fired among the people' at Goulceby, while William Doughty tells of 'many drunkards and dreadful persecution' at Swaby. Preachers at Holbeach were dragged off the chair and much abused, and the meeting house at Boston had to be made fast because of assailants.

53

LEFT: Hugh Bourne (1772-1852) and RIGHT: William Clowes (1780-1851) — chief leaders of the revival. CENTRE: Scotter first P.M. chapel where the 1829 Conference was held. (DNR) BELOW: Grimsby old market place where Thomas King preached.

ABOVE: Grantham market cross where Wedgwood preached. (DNR)
LEFT: Grimsby's first P.M. chapel in Loft Street. (DNR) CENTRE: John Wedgwood. (DNR) RIGHT: John Stamp, who was in Louth 1838-40. (DNR)

ABOVE: Louth P.M. chapel, 1850. (DNR)
BELOW: First and second P.M. chapels, Boston.
(DNR)

RIGHT: A group of Grimsby P.M. chapels. (DNR) ABOVE: First Lincoln P.M. chapel in Portland Place, 1839. (DNR) CENTRE: Second P.M. chapel, Lincoln. (DNR) BELOW: Kendall Memorial chapel, Ashby, 1885. (DNR)

57

ABOVE: Messingham P.M. chapel, 1846 with Sunday School added 1871.
(DNR) LEFT: First P.M. chapel, Alford. (DNR) RIGHT: Second P.M.
chapel, Alford, 1856. (DNR) BELOW: William Neal's house at Broughton
where Primitive Methodism began in the village. (DNR)

LEFT: Interior of Gainsborough Trinity Street P.M. chapel, 1878. (LE) RIGHT: Smethurst Memorial in Grimsby's People's Park. (DNR) BELOW: Laughton P.M. chapel, 1826. (DNR)

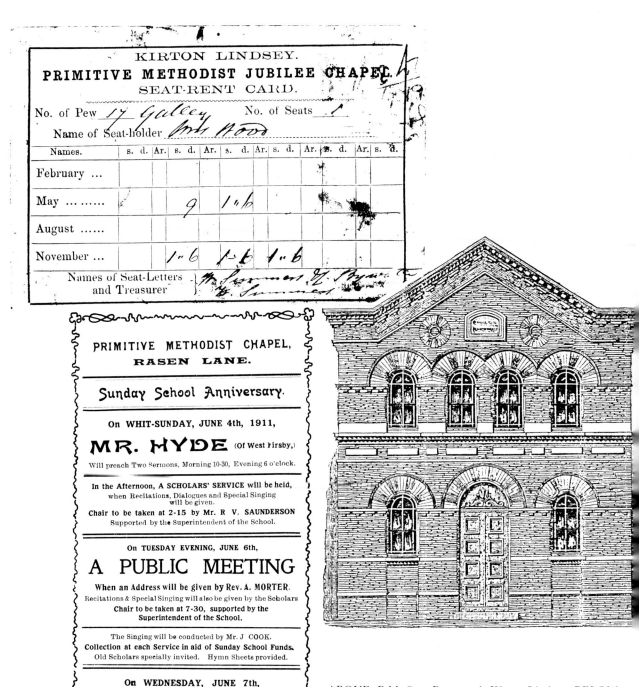

KIRTON LINDSEY.

PRIMITIVE METHODIST JUBILEE CHAPEL.

SEAT-RENT CARD.

No. of Pew *17 Galley*   No. of Seats *1*

Name of Seat-holder *Mrs Wood*

Names.	s. d.	Ar.	s. d.	Ar.	s. d.	Ar.	s. d.	Ar.	s. d.	Ar.	s. d.
February ...											
May			9	1 " 6							
August											
November ...			1 " 6	1 " 6	1 " 6						
Names of Seat-Letters and Treasurer											

PRIMITIVE METHODIST CHAPEL,

RASEN LANE.

Sunday School Anniversary.

On WHIT-SUNDAY, JUNE 4th, 1911,

MR. HYDE (Of West Firsby,)

Will preach Two Sermons, Morning 10-30, Evening 6 o'clock.

In the Afternoon, A SCHOLARS' SERVICE will be held,
when Recitations, Dialogues and Special Singing
will be given.
Chair to be taken at 2-15 by Mr. R V. SAUNDERSON
Supported by the Superintendent of the School.

On TUESDAY EVENING, JUNE 6th,

A PUBLIC MEETING

When an Address will be given by Rev. A. MORTER.
Recitations & Special Singing will also be given by the Scholars
Chair to be taken at 7-30, supported by the
Superintendent of the School.

The Singing will be conducted by Mr. J COOK.
Collection at each Service in aid of Sunday School Funds.
Old Scholars specially invited. Hymn Sheets provided.

On WEDNESDAY, JUNE 7th,

The Children will have their ANNUAL TEA at 4 p.m.

A PUBLIC TEA

Will be provided in the school-room from 4-30 to 6. 6d. each.
After Tea, the scholars will have their Games, etc., in a
Field on Burton Road, corner of the Extension, kindly lent
by Mr. Spurr. Admission to the Field, 1d. each.

ABOVE: P.M. Seat Rent card, Kirton Lindsey. BELOW: Rasen Lane P.M. Sunday School Anniversary, Lincoln, 1911. RIGHT: Market Rasen P.M. chapel, 1866. (DNR)

LEFT: Parkinson Milson (1825-93). RIGHT: The last P.M. Class Ticket, August 1932. CENTRE: William Byron of Louth, who gave £1,000 to the 1837 P.M. Conference. (DNR) BELOW: P.M. Class Ticket, 1910.

THE

Primitive Methodist Connexion

TO THE INHABITANTS OF

NEW YORK

AND OF THE

UNITED STATES OF AMERICA

IN GENERAL, SEND GREETING.

Friends and Brethren,

THE LORD having in his Providence raised up the Primitive Methodist Connexion, in Old England, and made it an instrument, in his hands, of turning thousands and ten thousands unto righteousness, and many of its members having emigrated to the United States, it was judged providential to appoint a regular **Mission.** We have accordingly sent over our respected Brother and faithful Minister, the Rev. WILLIAM KNOWLES; as also our respected Sister, RUTH WATKINS, who has laboured much in the LORD. And we trust they will be made useful in the Gospel of our common LORD, and will meet with that kindness and respect among you, that you, under similar circumstances, would expect from us.

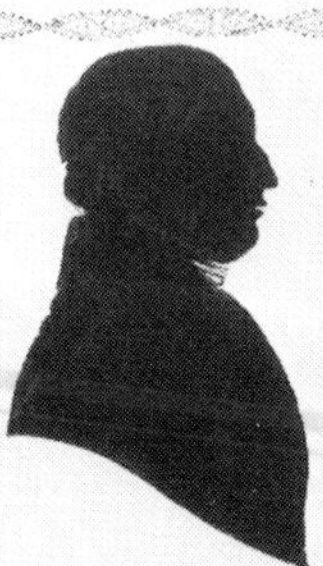

Signed in behalf of the Conference of the said Connexion,

James Bourne, **President.**

Hugh Bourne, **Secretary.**

ABOVE: Scotter P.M. Conference 1829, which OPPOSITE: sent missionaries William Knowles and Ruth Watkins to the U.S.A. BELOW: P.M. Louth Tee-total plan, 1839. (DNR)

LOUTH CIRCUIT, TEE-TOTAL

PRIMITIVE METHODIST PREACHERS' PLAN.

LORD'S DAY PLAN.

1839 PLACES AND TIME.		April 21	April 28	May 5	May 12	May 19	May 26	June 2	June 9	June 16	June 23	June 30	July 7	July 14
Louth	10	3	9	4	38	5	21	20	11	2	11	3	6	1c
	2	6	1	46	5	31	1c	19	26	31	3	10	1	26
	6	3	1s	4	5	5	1c	18	2	2	3	3	1	1c
Do. Sun. School and open Air	[illegible]	17	18	4	19	5	21	32	35	2	38	36	18	1
	[illegible]	17	18	10c	19	29	21	32	31	36	38	46	18	19
Legbourn	10		4		5		1c		2		3		1	
	6	10	6	18	16	9	11c	38s	22	23	27	31	14	45
Cockerington	2		7		4c		9		11		16L		12	
	6	11		6		14 c		10		1		2		3s
Alvingham	2	3		6L		5c		10		1		2		3
	6	16	47	31	4	18 c	9	14	11	35	16s	21	12	31
Saltfleetby	2	45	5L	19	6	10	5c	21	1	11	2s	9	3	25
	6	8	27	P	12	35	33 c	P	12	15	13	11	P	8
Saltfleet	6	45	3	19	6	10	5	21	1	11	2	9	3	7
Trusthorpe	10		5		51		2		3c		1		5	
	6	18		35		46		22		39 c		19		10
Mablethorpe	2	18	5L	35	14 c	16	2c	22	3s	39	1	19	5	10
	6		51		8		7c		13		52		40	
Theddlethorpe	10		51		14		7c		8		12		51	
	2	29		38		22L		31		10		38		35
	6	20	5	38	11 c	23	2c	31	3	10	1	38	5s	35
Grainthorpe	2	5		1cs		2 ms		3		18		5L		4
	6		14		36		46		31		33		13	
Somercotes	[illegible]	22	11	[illegible]	18 c	8	46	12	31	16	9	36	10	51
	[illegible]	[illegible]	13	1c	18	2	22	3	46	16	9	5	10	4

"For here have we no continuing city but we seek one to come. A Stranger in a strange land. I am as a wonder unto many; but thou art my strong refuge."

Names and Residences.

1 [illegible], Chapel House,
2 Bell, Alford,
3 Hutchinson, Hogsthorpe,
4 Procter, Louth,
5 Hewitt, do.

WEEK NIGHT PLAN.

PLACES AND NIGHT.	Apr. 22	Apr. 29	May 6	May 13	May 20	May 27	June 3	June 10	June 17	June 24	July 1	July 8	July 15
Somercotes ... m	5		13	Dis. Meetg.	2t				1		5		4
Grainthorpe ... t	5		9		sm				1		5		4
Saltfleet ... w	5		12		2t				1		5		4
Saltfleetby ... th	5		15		2t			ss	1		5		4
Reston ... f	5		56		2t				1		5		4
Theddlethorpe ... m		5		8		2t	Miss. meetg.		Week	1		5	
Trusthorpe ... t		5		55		2t				1		5	
Mablethorpe ... w		5		7		2t		3		1		5	
Markby ... th		5		29		2t		3		1		5	
Alford ... f		5		56		2t		3		1		5	
Bilsby ... m	4		5t		1c				3		1		5
Beesby ... t	4		5t		1c				3		1		5
Withern ... w	4		5t		1c				3		1		5
Legbourn ... th	4		5		1t				3		1		5
Burwell ... f	4		5		1t				3		1		5
Fotherby ... m		4		5		1t			Conference	[illegible]		1	
Louth ... t		4		5		1t				[illegible]		1	
Welton ... w			5t					2				1	
River-Head ... th		4		5		1t		2		3		1	
Alvingham ... f		4		5		1t		2		3		1	
Scamblesby ... m	3		1t		5				2		3		1
Louth ... t	3		4t		5				2		3		1
Kelstern ... w	3c				5t				2				1
Ludborough ... th	3		4t		5				2		3		1
Utterby ... f	3		4t		5				2		3		1
Grimoldby ... m		3		4t		5t				[illegible]		3	
Cocker[illegible] ... t		3		4t		[illegible]				[illegible]		[illegible]	

YORKS

Hull

NORTH SEA

Barton

Humber

GRIMSBY

Marshland

Crowle

Brigg

Epworth

SCOTTER

Scrooby

Gainsborough

Market Rasen

Louth

Alford

LINCOLN

Horncastle

Spilsby

MAP OF SCOTTER DIST. 1821.

BELOW: Map of Scotter P.M. District 1821. (DNR)

63

SCOTTER CIRCUIT.

TRAVELLING AND LOCAL PREACHERS' SUNDAY PLAN,

OF THE PEOPLE CALLED

Primitive Methodists:

Known also by the Name of RANTERS.

"THE LORD HATH DONE GREAT THINGS FOR US, WHEREOF WE ARE GLAD."—Psalm 126, iii v.

1821. Places.	Time		MAY 6	13	20	27	JUNE 3	10	17	24	JULY 1	8	15	22	29	AUGUST 5	12	19	26	SEPTEMBER 2	9	16	23	30	OCTOBER 7	14	21	28
Scotter	9	6	1	T4	12	5	c3	6	L2	14	4	23	6	2	5	14	c3	19	T1	25	5	L3	6	4	2	4	25	5
Messingham	1½		1	4	12	5	c3	6	2	14	L4	23	6	2	5	14	c3	19	T1	25	5	3	6	L4	2	4	25	5
Gainsbro'	2	6	4	2	16	T1	8	c5	23	3	12	9	4	11	1	23	5	16	T3	2	11	c4	8	5	1	9	4	5
Corringham	2		L2		35		33		11		32		21		33		9		8		L3		35		11		21	
Kirton	2	6	3	21	T5	14	23	c1	8	L4	20	19	2	21	7	3	8	5	10	19	c1	15	13	L5	3	11	2	
South Kelsey		6		36		3		19		28		36		9		36		17		8		20		9	3			
North Kelsey	2			36		L3		19		28		36		9		36		17		28		8		20		9	L3	
Willoughton	2		9	33	36	35	19	L2	21	17	25	8	9	36	11	55	19	24	36	17	12	36	L1	19	28	35	13	11
Waddingham	2				19		36		9		17		8		19		36		9		17		0		36		8	
Bishop Norton		6	8		19		36		9		17		8		19		36		9		17		26		36		8	
West Ferry	1½	6	14	L1	4	16	15	23	c3	2	19	29	3	4	21	5	L1	35	14	13	8	c2	4	1	29	5	16	3
Gunthorp		6	32		21		16		25		21		30		15		32		24		29		33		16		29	
East Lound	10			15		23		25		16		30		23		32		12		16		33		30		25		32
Burnham	2			15		23		25		16		30		23		32		12		16		33		30		25		32
Epworth	2		23	12	30	11	P	21	L1	12	11	14	16	15	12	25	12	30	5	7	23	11	34	25	4	30	7	L1
Haxey		6	23		30		15		1		11		16		12		15		L5		23		34		4		7	L1
Westwoodside	2	6	12		25		14		30	L5	34		12		15	4	32		25		2		30		L1			
Wildsworth	2			16		4		12		30		21		7	2L		11		25		32		7		21	15		12
East Ferry		6		16		L4		12		30		21		7	2		11		25		32		7		21	L1		12
Laughton	2			19		29		11	5	35		32		16		30		29		35	2	21		32		29		16
Blyton		6		19		29		11	5	35		32		16		50		29		35	L2	21		32		29		16
Misterton	2			29		32		33		21		16		30		33		16		32		16		23		21	5	
East Stockwith	2		29		1		30		12		29		32		23		16		12	5	33		28		25		32	
West Stockwith		6	29		1		30		19		29		32		23		16		12	5	33		29		25		32	
Belton	2	5	11	1	23	12	P	L3	7	4	23	25	30	14	4	11	34	15	30	12	14	15	L2	12	11	30	14	
Scotton	2			11			32		15		35	7		35		21		29		50		44		15		33		
Flixbro'	9	6	18	T3	24	c2	7	22	24	L1	18	4	24	3	22	31	18	c4	26	T1	24	18	8	31	22	2	14	4
Crosby	2		18	3	24	c2	7	22	24	1	18	L4	24	3	22	31	18	c4	26	T1	21	18	3	31	22	L2	14	4
Thealby	2		22		31		22		24		31		22		31		L2		24		31		P		24		26	
Thealby		6		18		24		31		26		18		24		26	2	26		22		18		31		22		
Burton	2		31		18		24		18		22		5		26		22		24	3		18		24				
Aulkbro'		6	31		18		24		18		22		5		26		18		22		24	L3		18		24		
Winterton	2		24		22		18	4	24		22		18		24		26		19		L5		22		24		31	
Halton		6	24		22		18	L4	24		22		18		24		26		18		5		22		24		31	
Ashby	2		26		9		17		22		11		26		18		26		31		9		14		26		18	
Brigg	2	6	5	10	T3	19	c2	18	4	9	24	L5	1	13	3	18	7	T2	c4	8	10	29	5	9	L3	17	2	18
Broughton	10		5	10	3	13	2	18	4	9	24	5	1	13	3	18	7	2	4	8	10	20	5	9	3	17	2	18
Cadney	2			20		28		17		19		20		28		17		36		27		24		10		13		28
Scawby	2		28	5		20		9		36		10		19		28		15	T2		36		9		17		9	
Hibaldstow		6	28	L5		20		9		36		10		19		28		13	2		36		9		17		9	
Bonby		6		13		10		13		10		13		10		13		31		24		10		28		22		13
Willoughby	2			13		10		13		10		13		10		13		31		24		10		28		22		13
Barnoldby	2		10		13		30		13		10		28		13		20		10		13		10				
Burringham	2		7		2		11		30		L5		14		25		30		15		26		29		14		12	
Butterwick		6	7		2		11		30		5		14		25		30		15		26		29		14		12	

Travelling Preachers.

1 S. Bailey.
2 W. Wombell.
3 W. Curtis.
4 Eliz. Bell.
5 — Bellam.
6 J. Oxtoby.

Local Preachers.

7 T. Harsley.
8 J. Wainwright.
9 J. Holingsworth
10 G. Storr.
11 J. Horberry.
12 Step. Jenkinson.
13 J. Parker.
14 J. Rusling.

Local Preachers on Trial.

15 J. Theaker.
16 Mary Barks.
17 Wm. Scott.
18 Jas. Neal.
19 F. Barrott.
20 W. Taylor.
21 S. Barnett.
22 J. Hobson.
23 J. Corringham.
24 Wm. Thornton.
25 G. Parkin.

Exhorters.

26 Thos. Levis.
27 J. Cooper.
28 Mary Moody.
29 Ann Lord.
30 D. Holmes.
31 B. Tupling.
32 Geo. Scott.
33 Wm. Farr.
34 Phb. Wrathmall.
35 Mary Fowler.
36 R. Walsham.

T. Tickets.
C. Collections.
S. Sacrament.
L. Love Feast.
C. M. Camp-Meetings.

Quarter-Days at Scotter, June the 17th and September 16th.——Local Preachers' Meeting to begin at Nine o'clock in the Morning of second day.—Business at Twelve o'clock. N. B. All Letters to be addressed to Benjamin Coolins, Scotton. Letters of Request must be post paid.

Any Preacher who cannot attend to his Appointments must himself get them supplied by one of the Preachers whose name is on the plan. It is expected that all those Preachers who are appointed within Five Miles of any Camp Meeting in this Circuit will repair to such Camp-Meetings to assist.—Let all the Exercises be short.

C.M. Westwoodside, June 3. C.M. at Scotter, July 8. C.M. at Brigg, Aug. 5. C.M. at Thealby, Sept. 9. C.M. at Gainsbro', July I. C.M. at Grayingham, July 22. C.M. at Epworth, Aug 19.
No. 1, 4, 5.   I, 2, 3,   I, 2, 4.   I, 4.   I, 2, 3.   I, 5, 6.   I, 3.

Scotter P.M. Circuit preaching plan, 1821.

Bricks and Mortar

Primitive Methodists were generally recruited from the poorer classes, and this is reflected in a number of events in the early days of the movement. It is especially evident in the type of building which housed the first generation of people. The society at Fulletby met in the house of Robert Fletcher, known locally as the champion thatcher. He had been appointed the first class leader and was a fluent speaker. The few members tried hard to find money for a chapel and, when at last they saw the way open, they were careful to declare it must be of little expense. When at last it was built there was a debt on it for which the company struggled heroically to find interest.

The first chapel at Goulceby was damp and uncomfortable and had a brick floor. There was no chapel at Grimoldby for over thirty years and no prospect of having one, solely on the grounds of expense. When at last the way became clear and 'after much prayer', the chapel was opened with a debt of £95 and for years this burden remained. The best that the members at Sibsey could do was to rent a mud and stud chapel, built by one of the members at his own expense and on his own land. There was a certain prophetic helplessness in the text inscribed over the door of the second chapel: 'Hitherto hath the Lord helped us'.

At Waltham the first room is described as 'low, badly ventilated and inconvenient'; it was rented for £4 a year. At Stickney the first room was built of inferior materials which soon deteriorated; the roof fell in and the members then returned to a small cottage. All hope of restoration was gone for, not only did the society disintegrate, but the few who remained had to recover the money to pay for the chapel, which was only a heap of rubble.

It is not surprising there were struggles in a cause which was largely composed of the labouring poor. The struggles are a remarkable testimony to the survival of many causes. It was one thing to have come into an experience which changed the lives of so many; it was another thing finding money to erect chapels in which to share that experience. Opposition was a mild thing compared with the difficulties they encountered when it came to chapel building. Groups were raised up in the flush of revival and it never occurred to these early Primitive Methodists that they might foster their newfound faith in the existing Wesleyanism. It was a different Methodism in some ways, and it called for a different home. For years they met in the cottages of a leader, always in the hope that they, like the Wesleyans, could have a chapel. Most of them were built with an exuberance of faith and a deficiency of money. The struggles went on for years for, added to the local expense, there was the need to find a stipend for the travelling preacher. But first in the minds of the members was the provision of a permanent place for worship.

Few stories rival the case at Amcotts where 'for more than thirty years our people have worshipped in a small house, which has much retarded the progress of the society. Repeated efforts have been made to obtain a site of land on which to erect a chapel; these efforts, however, proved abortive, and the friends have become so disappointed as to believe they could never succeed'.

A similar story is told of the society at Barnetby, where 'our people have laboured long with little success, partly from want of a better place of worship, and partly through dissolution and lukewarmness of the society'. At South Kelsey 'the little flock struggled for years'. Progress towards securing a chapel was not merely for want of money, but 'the owner of the village at that period was a very high churchman, and he would not grant them a site'. Kirkby on Bain 'suffered from the inconvenience of worshipping in an old mud dwelling', and the society 'being composed entirely of the labouring class, shrank from the task'. There is something resolute in the minute which the society at Kirkstead agreed upon: 'That there be a chapel at Kirkstead if the way open'; but the way did not open for nearly twenty years afterwards.

At Thorpe Bank in the fens the preachers made frequent attempts to keep the cause alive and 'the place has been repeatedly taken on and off the plan, generally for want of a suitable place in which to worship'. At Wainfleet there was long delay 'until Mrs Thornelly's garden was thought of, a portion of which she kindly offered', but this had to receive the landlord's consent, which was fortunately given.

Forty years of determination and effort lay behind the establishment of a cause at Great Gonerby. The 'cause languished, very few persons regularly attended; for the friends were greatly discouraged, and had it not been for the piety and perseverance of an honoured female, the wife of the parish clerk and village schoolmaster, it is probable the place would have been removed from the plan'. A barn was rented and, after more struggle, the longed-for chapel was erected.

Debts on many were heavy and prolonged over many years. Donington chapel cost £295, and a debt of £272 remained on it at the opening. West Quadring cost £160 to build and a debt of £130 was still outstanding when it was opened. Pinchbeck West cost £231 and only £6 was received at the opening service. This was typical of most of the county. Gedney Drove End was at one time required to find £60 in one year to prevent the chapel being sold. Many relied on money-lenders who asked no interest. Finance caused many a headache and long meetings of searching discussion. Perhaps the best example of resolving the money problems is contained in the minute of one chapel: 'That we borrow £120 from Mr Veal to pay back the £110 we borrowed from Mr Hack with interest, which he lent us to pay back the £100 we borrowed from Mr Jowett with interest'. Or, if that method did not have the required result, perhaps the minute of another chapel set a pattern for future finance meetings: 'That the committee will sit until it discovers a way of making our expenses come within our income'. One wonders how long the sitting lasted . . .

The Donington Circuit Quarterly Meeting report sums up much of the prevalent problems in the whole county: ' . . . struggle, struggle, which lasted for nearly thirty years'. Thirty years! This means that, by the time of the hungry forties, the Primitive Methodists were still in dire straits, and yet they had increased remarkably in numbers and influence, and had not only survived, but were confident of progress.

Primitive Methodism, like the Wesleyans, was largely the fruit of local people. The itinerant ministers did noble work, it is true, but the effort and dedication of quite ordinary people of quite outstanding ability gave the cause an impetus. Many of these people had little education and, while some remained in their own locality to spend a lifetime in the good work, others travelled more widely. They had all caught the spirit of the circuit system and the connexional ethos.

George Rex of Gainsborough tramped miles as a preacher, but his influence in his own town was such that he became the leading spirit in setting up a progressive cause in Spring Gardens, and started a Sunday school. Richard Keightley gave fifty years of excellent service to the village of Appleby, and also gave two sons to the full time ministry. Parkinson Milson, born and brought up in Broughton, a tree feller by occupation, until a narrow escape from death led to a remarkable conversion, became a full time minister. Atkinson Smith of Scotter, a farm foreman at

Messingham, is noted for the numerous testimonies of his prayers and their effectiveness in bringing about revivals. His brother, Edward, became a missionary to the United States of America. Indeed, the Scotter circuit was reported as having sent 'over twenty men into the ministry and several of them have high connexional position'.

But the Scotter Circuit was remarkable for other things, for its missioning enterprise extended over a wide area, including the Channel Isles. The first chapel to be erected was in 1819 and, within ten years of its being opened, the Primitive Methodists met there in Conference, when two momentous decisions were made. One was the signing of the Deed Poll, declaring the movement as a Connexion, only a year after Hugh Bourne despaired of the future of the whole work. The other decision was the appointing of Ruth Watkins and William Knowles as missionaries to America.

The Primitive Methodists employed a number of women itinerants. Elizabeth Lingard was known throughout the north of the county and had 'spiritual children all around her, and not a few of them preachers and class leaders'. Sarah Moody preached 'the gospel with great point and force, in a way calculated to make sinners tremble and saints rejoice'. Mary Birks, a native of Stockwith, served the Lincoln circuit for a few years, and she was deemed suitable to reinforce the American mission but, when interviewed by William Clowes, she declined.

Ann Tinsley followed Mary Birks in Lincoln and she in turn was succeeded by Elizabeth Swinton, a native of Swinderby and of gypsy clan, whose appearance in the pulpit in white with Quaker bonnet caused quite a stir. 'She was in the habit of visiting the villages during the annual feasts . . . and poured upon the people the awful truths of the divine word'.

The circuit system evolved in Primitive Methodism in much the same way as it had done among the Wesleyans and soon every town and many villages had their headquarters. Chapels sprang up everywhere, distinguished from their Wesleyan neighbours by the title only, and many bore a datestone over the door.

There was one travelling preacher in the county, John Stamp, who counted his success in terms of the number of chapels he had opened in the period 1835-1838. His wife, too, was an ardent evangelist. Louth was one of the wickedest places he visited, but 'hundreds of people' listened to him and his wife in the street. At Legbourne the 'chapel would not contain the people, so my wife spoke to hundreds in a schoolroom in the chapel yard'.

When it came to chapels, he laid the foundation stones in the presence of large crowds and preached repeating the same when they were opened. His self-opinionated diary gives a summary of his successes and the membership increases which resulted from his ministry. 'During three years . . . we have built sixteen chapels, enlarged one, bought another, and fitted up a large room, and had an increase of twenty-five local preachers and 416 members . . . ' When he left Louth he 'felt more strong to labour' than when he started.

Most of the chapels reflect the character of the movement. They were small, almost square, with a doorway to the road and four sash windows. Inside they had several rows of seats, rising by steps to the rear with centre aisle, box pulpit and a platform to the side, designed as 'singers' corner, later housing the harmonium. Brick floors gave way to wooden ones. A coke stove eventually provided much heat; lighting passed through the sequence of candle, gas and more recently electricity.

The chapels in the towns were modest at first, somewhat larger than the villages, and all giving way eventually to styles appropriate to the period. Some indeed were quite magnificent, after the early utilitarian structures. Boston built in George Street and then moved to a more prominent site in West Street. Lincoln had a squat chapel in Portland Place, replaced it by a more lofty chapel, and then moved into the High Street. Brigg built rather splendidly in the main street, a chapel seating 400 people. Epworth was built by subscription. 'The preachers went from house to

house begging and a hearty old farmer would go into the ale house too and it was astonishing how the money came rolling in and the Epworth people got up the Ranter's chapel'.

Grantham was perhaps the first to have a gallery, although the dimensions hardly warranted it. John Stamp's chapel at Louth had a gallery at one end. Sleaford purchased a large house in Westgate and 'we got it comfortably fitted up with seats and a pulpit', while the Loft Street chapel in Grimsby had formerly been in possession of an Independent group. Market Rasen had to be satisfied with a disused Wesleyan chapel.

Landowners were more amenable to the Methodists, be they Wesleyans or Primitives, providing in many instances land on a 99 years' lease. Lord Yarborough made it possible for the society at Habrough to build, and at Keelby the members got up a petition signed by twenty-four parishioners, some of whom were 'respectable farmers'. Major Amcotts gave land in his own village and Sir Montague Cholmeley helped the folk at Burton Coggles, whilst H. Heeley Esq of Ashby not only gave land, but 5,000 bricks for a chapel at Burringham. George Skipworth Esq leased land at South Kelsey, and Sir Culling Bardley did the same at Nettleton, as also the Earl of Dysart at Great Ponton. At Ashby, near Scunthorpe, it was 'our old friend, Francis Belton', who gave land, while 'a gentleman of the parish, James Scroby', provided for the people at Belchford.

In some villages the donor was a Methodist himself, one such being 'Mr Briggs who gave land and kindly superintended the building to great advantage'. John Smithson of Corringham was 'an old Primitive' and naturally aided the work in his own village. William Sharp of Holton le Clay, along with Mary, his wife, were among the first members in the village and, having sheltered the society in their home, also provided the plot of ground for the chapel. Richard Handeley of Irby in the Marsh gave land and a sovereign and promised two thousand bricks and a cauldron of lime. His action prompted others to give their sovereign and their labours. 'There was scarcely a house but gave something towards the chapel'.

And thus it grew. By the middle of the 19th century the Primitive Methodists numbered more than 7,000, with something like two hundred societies. Consolidated into a connexion, the Primitive Methodists stood four square with their Wesleyan neighbours.

OPPOSITE: *Wesleyan country chapels* — ABOVE LEFT: Hardwick, 1840.
RIGHT: Horsington, 1838. BELOW LEFT: Bonby, 1813. RIGHT:
Authorpe, 1862. *Pillared town chapels*. ABOVE: Hannah Memorial, 1864 on
Lincoln High Street. (LCL) BELOW: Boston Wesleyan — old (1839) and
new (1911). (DNR)

WESLEYAN CHAPEL, BOSTON.

THE OLD   THE NEW

ABOVE: The old Boston Wesleyan on fire 29 June 1909,
BELOW: and the gutted interior. (All DNR) RIGHT: The new
interior.

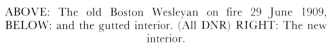

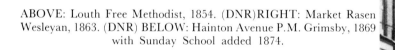

ABOVE: Louth Free Methodist, 1854. (DNR)RIGHT: Market Rasen
Wesleyan, 1863. (DNR) BELOW: Hainton Avenue P.M. Grimsby, 1869
with Sunday School added 1874.

ABOVE: Lincoln Wesley, 1836, in Clasketgate. (DNR)
Chapels with spires — RIGHT: Epworth Wesley Memorial,
1889 and BELOW: the interior (Both DNR)

Trinity Wesleyan Church.
STAMFORD.

LEFT: Opening of Woodhall Spa Wesleyan on Broadway, August 1907.
(WC) RIGHT: Trinity Wesleyan, Stamford, 1886.

73

ABOVE: Cleethorpes Trinity Wesleyan, 1885.
(DNR) BELOW: St Catherines, Lincoln, 1880.
(LCL)

Other town chapels — ABOVE: Finkin Street, Grantham, Wesleyan 1841.
BELOW: Interior of Flottergate, Grimsby, P.M. 1880. (DNR)

ABOVE: Louth Riverhead chapel, 1849. BELOW: — taken down and rebuilt at Theddlethorpe All Saints in 1855. (Both DNR) RIGHT: Interior of Horncastle Wesleyan. 1870. (DNR)

ABOVE: Sleaford Wesleyan chapel and Manse, 1848. (DNR) BELOW: Gosberton Wesleyan (Salem), 1878. (DNR) LEFT: Bailgate, Lincoln, 1880.

ABOVE: Messingham Wesleyan, 1821. LEFT: — and the organ decorated for the harvest festival in 1906. (both DNR). RIGHT: Interior of Alford Wesleyan a few years after opening in 1865.

78

Reform

There were two secessions from Wesleyan Methodism. The first was in 1797, and led to the formation of the Methodist New Connexion the other was the result of more widespread agitations in the early 1850s, which led to the creation of the United Methodist Free Churches. Both events were attempts to liberate the Wesleyan church from the dominating power of the Conference, and to set up a more democratic form of church government.

In Lincolnshire the area of Methodist New Connexion influence was confined almost exclusively to the Isle of Axholme, with small offshoots in Gainsborough and Scotter, and an autonomous, yet very vigorous cause in Boston. The demand for liberty and a wider representation of laymen in the government of the church was led by Alexander Kilham, himself an Epworth man, and it is therefore not surprising that Epworth should have been the first place to embrace the principles of reform he advocated.

Most of the support for Kilham and his reforms came from the new industrial towns of the North and Midlands. Kilham was one of Wesley's preachers, a young man with large vision and an enterprising spirit. His reform pamphlets were revolutionary, and his publication of these led to his expulsion from the Wesleyan church in 1796. This somewhat startling event naturally aroused the sympathy of his family, and he was soon back in Epworth, where he preached several times in the chapel: 'Mr Robinson, the superintendent, either conniving at it or going out of town to afford him opportunity of doing so in his absence'.

In August 1797 a small band of ministers and laymen assembled in Ebenezer chapel in Leeds and constituted the first conference of the New Connexion, as it was to be known. In November the same year, a New Connexion preacher was appointed to Epworth, and soon several societies were joined to form a circuit. In December 1798 Kilham died, but what he had initiated gained ground and, after twenty-five years, had twenty-five circuits and over 10,000 members.

The effect on the Wesleyan membership was less pronounced than might appear, and the disruption was in some areas insignificant. In Epworth the Wesleyan membership dropped from 957 to 600, but the gains to the New Connexion were only 150. It would therefore seem that the disruption led to a large number ceasing membership altogether. There was another problem too in Epworth. It concerned the chapel. Most of the trustees had transferred their allegiance to Kilham and the question arose as to the rightful owners. For a period the chapel was shared 'either preaching alternately on the Sabbath or otherwise at different hours'. In 1803 the New Connexion was forced to withdraw and, after worshipping in a barn and then in Simon Kilham's house, they built a chapel. They also moved in to one or two other villages. The prospects were good. A Sunday school was started in Thomas Kilham's shop, and many tradesmen in the town learned to read and write there.

When the school came to its jubilee in 1854 the occasion was used to launch a scheme for a new building, and £78 was raised in a large meeting held in the Court House. The scheme became a concern of the whole connexion. John Nelson 'was authorised to traverse the length and breadth of the Connexion, soliciting subscriptions for the accomplishment of this object'. The effort was a great success, and the new chapel, a gothic structure, and an 'ornament to the Connexion' was built in memory of Kilham.

The work extended to Eastoft, Westwoodside, Craiselound and Haxey. The cause established in Gainsborough was short-lived, but the one at Scotter had a longer life and, taking over the old Primitive Methodist chapel, they soon became a formidable society.

The origin of the movement in Boston lies in obscurity, but a splinter group from the Wesleyans met in a room in Angel Court, and by 1827 they numbered 66 members with a minister in charge. In 1829 they built their 'Zion' chapel in West Street. Something of the strength of this group is reflected in their spending £2,000 in the 1830s on a variety of projects, and doubling their membership. The society was composed of a mixed group in the town — shop-keepers, coal-merchants, fishmongers, millers, bakers and hairdressers. Harry Broughton was a music teacher in Tower Street. The lower classes were well represented.

A small attempt to establish a New Connexion cause in Louth had every prospect of success, for in 1898 John Naull wrote to Kilham telling him that there were 'several in Louth who are favourable to your interest and who have nowhere to attend divine worship, but with the old connexion, and these treat him as vassals . . .'. He appealed for a zealous man to be sent, and to give emphasis to the need said the town 'had near 7,000 inhabitants, many of whom are much inclined to hear the gospel'. He said there was but one 'steeple house', and a Methodist chapel, 'much too small'. It all came to nothing; perhaps the death of Kilham led to the demise of the cause.

The second attempt at reform came in the early 1850s. Since the events of 1797, there had been other movements in the Wesleyan connexion which had challenged the authority of the main body: one was known as the Leeds Organ case of 1827, another surrounded the problems over the establishment of a Theological College in 1834. Neither caused anything more than a ripple in Lincolnshire.

The year 1849 has gone down in Methodist history as the greatest upheaval within the Wesleyan church. It was all sparked off by the distribution of anonymous 'fly-sheets', the publication of *The Wesley Banner*, and the expulsion of three Ministers — James Everett, William Griffith and Samuel Dunn. It brings to light those 'old, unhappy, far off things, and battles long ago'. It all began with what one historian called 'the paper war'.

The agitation covered a period of two or three years before the real storm broke, and it was when the three chief agitators of reform were expelled by the Wesleyan Conference that the unrest almost turned into violence. First there was the indignant protest of the method of expulsion, then violent reaction against those who tried to suppress the agitators. Ministers and laymen joined in the fight for reform, but it was the laity chiefly, perhaps because of their greater numbers, who took the initiative. Everyone who espoused the principles of reform were charged with disloyalty and hastily dismembered. Class Meetings became minor inquisitions. Class tickets (those marks of membership and means of admission to love feasts and other meetings) were withheld; class books were confiscated by the ministers; leaders were dismissed from office. The problems were greatly increased when it came to trustees who took up the cause of reform, for they virtually held the keys to the chapels.

The movement snowballed, and soon hundreds were expelled from attending authorised meetings. Thousands of members were lost to the Wesleyan church, property was confiscated and many left the cause altogether. Between 1851 and 1856 Wesleyan Methodism was depleted by more than 100,000 members, which represented more than a quarter of the total membership of the whole church. In Lincolnshire the total loss was about 5,000, a similar percentage to the national figure.

After the expulsion of the three ministers, the circuits sought their services, first because they were connexional figures who became the best advocates for reform, but secondly their presence in the circuits gave added strength to those who were working for reform at local level. So they travelled the connexion. All three were in Louth in November 1849; Samuel Dunn preached in the Primitive Methodist chapel; James Everett spoke in the Mansion House, and William Griffith drew a large crowd to the Guildhall. A charge of 1s 6d was made for entry and over 600 people attended each of the three centres. It is said that Griffith spoke for over four hours.

When Griffith went to Market Rasen a marquee was erected to accommodate the thirteen hundred who attended. He spoke again for four hours and, as if that was not sufficient time to explain the principles of reform, several preachers gave verbal support. James Everett spoke at a meeting in the Corn Exchange at Lincoln 'to a densely crowded audience', and then went on to address an 'enthusiastic meeting' in the Corn Exchange at Gainsborough. He was the first reform speaker in Horncastle, where the Independent Chapel was hired for the occasion, resulting in 'an efficient committee' being formed. Enthusiasm ran high for the visit of Samuel Dunn who spoke to over a thousand in a malt kiln. In Spalding the reformers used the Assembly Rooms; in Grimsby a large warehouse, and a theatre in Grantham. The three visited all these towns, as well as Bourne, Brigg, Sleaford and Spilsby.

The movement started in the town chapels, where naturally large numbers gathered, but it spread to the villages, where in many instances there was a fair supply of local preachers who assured the timid that the cause was just and urgent. In some cases a whole society turned reform and the chapel ceased as a Wesleyan overnight. The areas most affected in the county were Lincoln, Louth, Market Rasen, Spalding, Grantham and Holbeach. Soon these towns were sending delegates to district meetings, and a strong contingent travelled to London to attend a national gathering.

Certain areas were affected little and it is interesting to see why. One district meeting passed a resolution 'that the friends of reform at Spilsby, Wainfleet, Bourne, Coningsby and Grimsby be offered assistance in getting up reform meetings at the earliest possible period'. These towns were the obvious weak spots. A statement from Coningsby reveals the nature of the caution: 'At the request of several local preachers and office bearers, I write to say that, although we had no delegate to represent our circuit, yet we are not indifferent to the cause of reform. Many of us deeply sympathise with the expelled ministers, disapprove of the proceedings of the late Conference and the manifesto issued by the President . . . The reason we have not occupied a more prominent position is on account of the smallness of our circuit and the kindness of our minister'. The last sentence gives a clue to why some circuits did not embrace the principles of reform as readily as others, for Seth Dixon, the minister at Coningsby, made very little of the agitation and allowed it to burn out.

Spilsby circuit reported that 'many, probably the majority of the circuit, are in favour of reform. There are a few sticklers for Conference, where minds are so much prejudiced that they will not be convinced. We have hitherto held our peace which is attributable to the conduct of our Ministers, who "think and let think", there is nevertheless, a strong undercurrent flowing which will, ere long, appear'. But it did not appear, for the Superintendent, Jonathan Cadman, had through all his ministry been 'doing quiet and effective work', and here also reform activity soon died out.

There are conflicting reports from Alford. One says 'the reform movement here is exhibiting signs of vigorous life', while another says 'things have gone somewhat smoothly here since Conference. Mr Eckersley is a peacemaker and Mr Armson has ceased for awhile, at least to be a peacebreaker'.

Much depended on the Ministers and their attitude to the agitators. Thomas Cocking succeeded Jonathan Cadman at Spilsby, equally as placid as his predecessor, and he had come from Barton upon Humber, where 'this circuit is considered very quiet owing principally to the mild role of the Superintendent, T. Cocking. There is, however, a strong undercurrent in favour of the reform movement and it will not be long before there is an outburst, as Mr Rouse is doing much towards rousing the people'. A play upon words, perhaps, but Nathan Rouse left Barton the following year and, with his departure, the reform spirit ceased.

The reformers made some attempt to gain a foothold in Grimsby and did in fact build a chapel in Freeman Street but, apart from a small mission cause in Cleethorpes, never made any great headway. When Ambrose Freeman, the Minister at Wainfleet, called a special meeting to discuss reform, and 'used all the means he could devise to abridge and cripple the resolution . . .' that put an end to any further activity. At Gainsborough 'a considerable portion of the society sympathise with them, [the three expelled ministers], but are unwilling to take any measures of a divisive character in the circuit'. There was little support. In Horncastle, after the first wave of enthusiasm, the cause died out.

However, the movement gained strength in Louth, Lincoln, Grantham, Spalding, Brigg, Market Rasen and Holbeach. These centres soon had large numbers as declared reformers, and there were spokesmen in quantity who convincingly swayed the majority. The chief spokesman in Louth was Alderman John Booth Sharpley, a corn merchant, prominent Wesleyan, and a member of a Connexional Committee, who had been Mayor on three occasions. When the Superintendent, James Loutit, withheld the tickets of 100 members the storm broke. His successor Richard Ray made an attempt to bring the agitators to order but when he read out the names of over 600 members who were known to have reforming sympathies, and who would be expelled if they did not make an individual promise to remain loyal to the cause, the die was cast.

The reformers soon organised themselves into a separate body, took the Baptist chapel as a preaching centre, and J.B. Sharpley presided at a service of Holy Communion. The Wesleyan schools in Newmarket and Lee Street were taken over and used for services. By December 1853 the Louth Reformers set up what they called the Free Methodist Chapel, that eight Corinthian-pillared 1,200 seater erection once so prominent in Eastgate, which chapel became known as 'the house that Jack built', as J B Sharpley lived right opposite, and he worshipped in it for the rest of his life. Working once so vigorously for the Wesleyan cause, he gave all his energies to the Free Methodist Chapel across the road.

The agitation in Lincoln resulted in the loss of some 300 members from the big Wesley chapel and the small Newport mission. The seceders took the old Zion chapel in Silver Street, after a period of worshipping in the Corn Exchange. The reformers in Boston met first in a disused chapel in Mainbridge and built in Pump Square. William Booth, later of the Salvation Army, ministered to the first reform congregation in Spalding. When the congregation built their chapel in The Crescent, they were a formidable body in that town.

The Louth 'Aggregate', a unique occasion in Methodism, was born after the parent church was so depleted by the 'split' that remaining Wesleyan members from all corners of the circuit gathered for mutual encouragement and inspiration. For many years it was an unwritten rule that the President of the Conference should preach, but the occasion still continues, on a Sunday and Monday in February, with leading preachers from the Connexion.

Holbeach in the fens embraced the reform spirit, and built in Albert Street. Grantham reformers experienced many trials of leaders before expulsion, but the result of these trials led them to carve out of the troubles a reform circuit based in the town. Brigg used the Forester's Hall until they erected a chapel in Bigby Street, and Market Rasen, while having a conscience in building so near the Wesleyans, nevertheless took a plot of ground in Union Street.

Reform Methodism led eventually to the creation of the United Methodist Free Churches in 1857, never a large body, and never wholly at variance with the Wesleyans, whom they had left so far as doctrine was concerned. But they provided a freedom in government which enabled the lay folk to take a more direct and important part in the life of the church, and this bore fruit in the production of many capable leaders and preachers.

ABOVE: Free Methodist singing competition at a Sunday School gala in Louth, 1911. (DNR) CENTRE: Rev Alexander Kilham (1762-98). (DNR) BELOW: Messingham P.M. Stonelaying of Sunday School, 1871. (HLS)

James Everett · William Griffith · Samuel Dunn

Thomas Knutsey

GAMEKEEPER,

WELL DIGGER, & VERMIN KILLER

BENNIWORTH,

Presents his grateful acknowledgements to his friends and the public, for the liberal support hitherto received, and wishes to inform them that he has added another branch to his already extensive Business, namely,---

BREAKING REFORM CHAPELS OPEN.

T. K. keeps a Conference Crow Bar in readiness, and pledges himself on the Shortest Notice and Lowest Possible Terms, to break open any Wesleyan Methodist Reform Chapel in this or any other Circuit.

Orders forwarded through the Rev. RICHARD WRAY will be promptly attended to.

OPPOSITE ABOVE: General William Booth, (white beard) in 1908; he was a Minister at Spalding in the Reform period. LEFT: Free Methodist seat rent receipt, Louth, 1871. RIGHT: Free Methodist Class Ticket, Louth 1889. BELOW: The three Reformers James Everett, William Griffith and Samuel Dunn were in Louth in November 1849. ABOVE: Handbill of Thomas Knutsey, Reform chapel breaker. (DNR)

NETTLEHAM

United Methodist Sunday School

ANNIVERSARY.

On SUNDAY, June 23rd, 1912,

TWO SERMONS will be preached by

Mr. H. W. COTTINGHAM

(OF BROXHOLME),

In the Morning at 10-30, and in the Evening at 6 o'clock.

In the Afternoon at 1-45, a

CHILDREN'S SERVICE

will be held, consisting of

RECITATIONS, DIALOGUES AND SINGING.

Collection after each Service in aid of Sunday School Funds.

On MONDAY, June 24th, 1912,

THERE WILL BE

A PUBLIC TEA provided in the Institute,

Tickets 6d., Children 3d. each, after which a

PUBLIC MEETING will be held in the Chapel.

Chair to be taken at 6-30 p.m.

OPENING
NEWMARKET
FREE METHODIST CHAPEL,
LOUTH.

On SUNDAY the 26th of JULY, 1868,

REV. T. HACKING,
OF HEYWOOD,

A LOVEFEAST

REV. J. GUTTRIDGE,
OF PRESTON,

Will preach in the FREE METHODIST CHAPEL, EASTGATE.

On MONDAY, JULY the 27th,

A PUBLIC TEA

Will be provided in the Newmarket School-Room, at Four o'clock. At Seven o'clock, a MEETING will be holden in the Chapel in Eastgate, when Addresses will be delivered by the Revs. J. GUTTRIDGE, M. MILLER, and J. MYERS.

MR. A. SHARPLEY, OF TORRINGTON, WILL PRESIDE.

On SUNDAY, AUGUST 2nd,

REV. J. KENDALL,
OF MANCHESTER,

REV. J. COLMAN,
OF SCARBOROUGH.

A Collection will be made at the Meeting, and at each Service (the last excepted) in aid of the Funds of Newmarket Chapel. At the last Service a Collection will be made towards defraying the Expenses of the Annual Assembly.

A STALL of USEFUL and FANCY ARTICLES will be provided in the Newmarket School-Room early in September. Articles suitable for sale would be thankfully received by Messrs. G. SLIGHT and S. SUTTON.

PRINTED BY W. SHEPHERD 5, MARKET-PLACE, LOUTH.

LEFT: Nettleham U.M. Sunday School Anniversary, 1912. RIGHT: Opening of Newmarket Free Methodist chapel, Louth in July 1868. (DNR) BELOW: Kilham Memorial chapel on High Street, Epworth, opposite the Wesley Memorial Chapel. (DNR)

FREE METHODIST
CHAPEL,
LOUTH

THE
FOUNDATION STONE
OF THE
New Chapel,

To be erected in Eastgate, will be laid

On THURSDAY, JULY 6th, 1854, by
J. B. SHARPLEY, Esq.,
AT HALF-PAST TWO O'CLOCK IN THE AFTERNOON.

The Members and Friends will take

TEA

together on MR. SHARPLEY'S LAWN, Eastgate, at Five o'clock;—should the weather prove unpropitious, arrangements will be made for Tea in in the CORN EXCHANGE.   A

PUBLIC MEETING

Will be held in the Evening; G. MALLINSON, Esq., from Huddersfield, D. WHITEHEAD, Esq., from Rawtenstall, W. MARTIN, Esq., from Manchester, and other Friends are expected to attend and take part in the proceedings.   All Friends of religious liberty are invited to attend.

TICKETS for Tea, 1s. each, may be had of Mr. Shepherd, Market-Place; Mr. J. Pearson, Butcher-Market; Mr. R. Hurley, Eastgate; Mr. R. Cross, New-Market; and Mr. T. Topham, River-Head.

Shepherd, Printer, Louth.

Stone laying poster for new Free Methodist chapel in Louth, 1854.

METHODIST NEW CONNEXION, EPWORTH.
Preachers' Entertainment Plan.

HOST.	GUEST.	DATE, 1894-5.
Mrs. Dawson	No 25	November 11th
Mrs. Needham	No. 14	~~January 24th~~
Mr. T. Lindley	No 19	January 13th.
Mr. Dempster	No. 24, 19	November 18th January 27th
Mr. T. Dawson	No 2, 2,	November 25, ~~December 2nd~~ January 6th.
The Manse	No 2	December 2nd
Mrs. Wells	No. 24	December 30th.
Mr Oliver	No. 4	December 9th

METHODIST NEW CONNEXION, EPWORTH.
Preachers' Entertainment Plan.

HOST.	GUEST.	DATE, 1895.
Mrs. Dawson	No 13	Feb 17.
Mrs. Needham	No. 25	April 21.
Mr. T. Lindley	No 27.	Mch 31
Mr. Dempster	No. 2	April 14.
Mr. T. Dawson	No 2	Mch 3.
The Manse	No 2	Mch 17. ~~April 14~~
Mrs. Wells	No. 16	Mch. 10th
Mr Oliver	No. 4	May 5th.

ABOVE: Methodist New Connexion Preachers' Entertainment plan, Epworth, 1894-5. OPPOSITE ABOVE: Louth Free Methodist Prayer Leaders' plan, 1875. BELOW: Muckton Bottom F.M. chapel, 1872, formerly Wesleyan. (DNR)

THE LOUTH FREE METHODIST PRAYER LEADERS' PLAN,

From September 5th, to December 26th, 1875.

PLACES.	HOUR	SEPT. 5	12	19	26	OCT. 3	10	17	24	31	NOV. 7	14	21	28	DEC. 5	12	19	26
Sun. Aft. & Evening.																		
Eastgate Chapel	2					2	3	4		6	7	8	1	2	3	7	8	6
	7½					2	1		5	7	6	8		2	5	1	4	6
Acthorpe	6									2	1	3	6	5	4	7	1	2
Elkington	2½																	
Keddington	6				7	1	6	5	4	3	8	7	2	1	3	6	5	8
Raithby	6					8	2	3	1	6	4	5	7	8	2	4	6	1
Welton Spring	6							7	8	5	2	4	8	6	1	5	3	7

NAMES OF PRAYER LEADERS.

1 Boothby, Gelsthorpe, England, Arliss, G. White.
2 Broadbent, Hudson, Strawson, Rhodes, Burkitt, Nundy.
3 Milligan, Codd, W. Dowse, Woodrow, G. Fowler, Birkett.
4 West, Sanderson, Coppin, White, Green, W. Burman.
5 Brown, Nicholson, Bradshaw, Wallis.
6 Frieston, Smurthwaite, Walster, T. Oakes, J. Wilson.
7 Hurton, R. Plaskett, Paddison, C. Oakes, Wright, Cuthbert.
8 Bryan, Sutton, Wilson, Farmery, I. Burt, Taylor.

Gurnell, *Supernumary*

All the Prayer Leaders present in the Louth Free Methodist Chapel, on Sunday Evenings, as well as those appointed on the plan, are requested to take their places within the communion rails at the close of the preaching service.

RULES FOR THE PRAYER LEADERS.

I.—The Secretary to be chosen at the Annual Meeting in December.

II.—That a Meeting of the Prayer Leaders be held the last Wednesday in every month, at which all are requested to attend; the first of each company is particularly requested to take or send a report of the attendance of his company, to each monthly meeting.

III—That any Prayer Leader reported to have neglected his appointments, shall be summoned to the next monthly meeting, to answer for such neglect, and that if he has not a sufficient reason to give, shall be admonished from the chair; and if he neglect three times without a sufficient reason, he shall cease to be on the plan.

IV.—That after any person has been approved of as a Prayer Leader he be not put on the plan until he has been seen and consented to go.

V.—That all Prayer Leaders in case of unavoidable absence shall provide a proper substitute.

JOSEPH MAWER, PRINTER, LOUTH.

LEFT: Boston West Street Methodist New Connexion chapel, 1828. BELOW: Silver Street F.M. chapel, Lincoln, 1864. (LCL) RIGHT: Rev William C. Jackson, President of the Conference 1935.

Victorian Elegance

Throughout the 19th century Methodism was divided — divided by denominational labels, all of which makes for some confusion for the modern historian, but not to the people who lived at the time. The aficionados of John Wesley remained loyal to the old body as it was called, the Wesleyan Church; although somewhat weakened by the disruptions of the 1850s, within two decades it had recovered much of its former strength. The Primitive Methodists, after a period of turmoil and struggle and uncertainty, made remarkable progress. The Methodist New Connexion, never strong in Lincolnshire, maintained a firm position in the Isle of Axholme and in Boston, but never extended its range of influence. The formation of the United Methodist Free Churches in 1857 was the consolidation of the reform movement of previous years, and was fairly progressive in Louth and Lincoln, but had circuits extending from Brigg to Holbeach.

The divisions were accepted. Members of all these denominations might work together in the fields and share in the industrial and business life of the towns, but on Sunday they went to their own chapel and on weeknights met in their own class meeting. In spite of this there was unity in diversity. There were in fact occasions when the unity took on practical expression; preachers went into neighbouring circuits, there were transfers from one denomination to another, and when new chapels were opened the speakers quite frequently included ministers from other denominations, including those of the other nonconformist chapels.

The Victorian period was the age of the big chapels in the towns. There were more people to accommodate, congregations were large and the first chapels became too small. The most notable and most elegant of these Victorian structures were Wesley Clasketgate in Lincoln with its Corinthian pillars, and Gainsborough Wesley which stood on the site of the new St Stephen's. Boston Centenary, the second of its kind, was as fine a building as any in the town; and there was Grantham Finkin Street, Grimsby George Street, and Sleaford Northgate, on the site of the modest building of recent days.

The opening of these were accompanied by a good deal of ceremony and, in addition to the large galleried chapel, they all included adequate accommodation for Sunday school work, which reached its peak before the century ended. The preacher at Boston for the opening of the first Centenary was Rev Thomas Jackson, who had been in the circuit as a young man, and was now the Connexional Editor and President of the Conference; and as if one star preacher was not enough, Dr Robert Newton, President in 1840, was also there. 'We certainly never witnessed anything like the intense interest this chapel created . . . the thousands that attended . . . the extraordinary collection — all contributed to render this one of the most important movements connected with Methodism that has ever taken place in Lincolnshire'. William Small, a young preacher, put the occasion into many verses:

'What noble building meets my eyes   Its turrets pointing to the skies,
With firm foundation laid -   Its massive colonnade'.

The motive which led the Grantham Methodists to leave their old chapel was on 'account of its being too small, as well as imperfectly ventilated, and containing but few seats for the poor'. Built in the Tuscan order, the new stood only a few yards down the road:

'It stands in Finkin Street,   The Philosophic Institute,
The centre of the town;   Stands rather lower down'.

They celebrated the opening with three weeks of services with star preachers and the building was almost paid for by the time it was opened, and 'it is but just to state that Mrs Guy of Plungar, has already given the sum of three hundred guineas towards the erection'. Young John Rogers recites it all in 72 verses:

'What splendid building this,
That rears its Front so grand?
Magnificent indeed it is,
And stately it doth stand.'

Sleaford Methodists purchased the old Falcon Inn for £1,500, to the annoyance of a legal gentleman who would have given double that amount had he known the Methodists were buying it. But soon the inn disappeared and Dr John Hannah preached the opening sermon. In Stamford the old chapel in Barn Hill was not 'a commanding site, being hidden by private residences', but the houses which hid it from view were purchased and the new chapel, a gothic structure, was built in front of the old, satisfying to the people who came in their carriages to hear that great missioner Hugh Price Hughes make 'an earnest and witty appeal for subscriptions' to clear off the remaining expense of building.

In Spalding the Methodists had had to be content with a chapel 'in a side street, and set back from the roadway, practically out of sight, and hemmed in by cottages, pig styes, stables, etc, which seemed to be the custom of Methodists in those days . . . ', but in 1886 they built quite grandly in Broad Street.

The Gothic and semi-Gothic were architectural types of the later Victorian period; some included a spire — such for example, the Wesley Memorial at Epworth, Trinity at Cleethorpes, Scunthorpe Centenary and Lincoln St Catherines. In the case of the last, the spire was an afterthought, for it was not erected until 1909, twenty years after the chapel was opened. Lincoln Bailgate, Spilsby and Skegness are fine examples of the semi-Gothic of the late Victorian era. Lincoln Silver Street stood more prominently than Wesley in Clasketgate, and in Grimsby the really big chapels were in Flottergate, Hainton Avenue and Garibaldi Street. Indeed, every town had its commodious chapel and they were all well attended, with many week-night activities going on in them all.

Victorian Methodists were sharply divided between rich and poor, although there were many members in the middle classes. The wealthy members paid for their pew by an annual rental and upholstered it to give it distinction. There were 'free' seats for the poor in all these big chapels. To meet the need of the poorer members as well as providing wider opportunities for active service, not always possible in the big buildings, the more wealthy made provision for them by setting up little mission chapels. This paternal gesture was never regarded as other than large generosity; it provided an outlet for the rich, and gave to the poor a place more suited to their social standing.

The folk at Lincoln Wesley opened a little mission hall in Well Lane and in Bagholme Road. Lincoln Bailgate opened a mission hall in Burton Road. At Barton upon Humber it was largely the initiative of one man, Mr Tombleson, who gave land and paid for a chapel at Waterside. In Grimsby the George Street Methodists build a little mission hall in King Terrace, and George Bett, brother to Dr Henry Bett, was the energetic leader for much of his life. Similarly a tin mission was erected in Alexandra Road. The Louth Methodists extended their work to the River Head, and Grantham pioneered a cause in Wharf Road. In Boston the Methodists at Centenary, perhaps less paternal, but with an eye to expansion, developed centres at Lincoln Lane, where John Hall established a Ragged School and Band of Hope. Hospital Bridge and Skirbeck were other areas of expansion, with an iron chapel in Brothertoft Road.

These offshoots of the parent body soon became self-supporting and offered opportunities for a wide variety of service, by people who otherwise would not have found an outlet for their talents: they stood equal with their richer neighbours'.

Wesleyan-Methodist Society,

ESTABLISHED 1739.

"CHRIST IS THE HEAD OF THE CHURCH."—*Eph.* v. 23.

High St.—Lincoln High St. Circuit.

Frank Wright

ADMITTED ON TRIAL, *May—* 1899.

E. H. *Minister.*

LEFT: Joseph Clarke signed the 1851 Religious Census form for Haven Bank. (HL) RIGHT: Wesleyan Class Ticket, admitted on trial, 1899. BELOW: Rules of the Wesleyan Mission Coffee House String Band.

RULES.

1—That the name of the Band shall be "The Coffee Hall Wesleyan Mission String Band."

2—That the President, Secretary, Treasurer, Conductor, with two members of the Band and two members of the Mission Committee, shall form a Committee of Management.

3—All members of the Band must also be Christians, members of a Christian Church, and play nothing but sacred music.

4—Candidates for admission shall be proposed and seconded by two members of the Committee, and carried or rejected by a majority of votes. Each member by joining the Band, binds himself to submit to the Rules and Regulations thereof.

5—No member shall play with another Band without the consent of the Bandmaster and Secretary.

6—If the conduct of any member shall be such as appears to the Committee to endanger the character of the Mission, it shall be in the power of the Committee to summon a special meeting to consider as to the expulsion of such member, half the Committee of Management, at least, to be present.

7—In all cases, where practicable, members shall purchase their own instruments; but when a member has the loan of an instrument from the Committee, if he withdraw, or is expelled from the Band, he shall at once return the same.

8—That all property of the Band be vested with the Mission Committee for the time being.

9—All applications for engagements to be made to the Secretary, and decided by the Committee, except in special cases, with which the Bandmaster and Secretary shall have power to deal.

10—Each member shall affix his or her signature to the above Rules, in a book provided for the purpose, and shall be supplied with a printed copy of the same.

ABOVE: Sturton by Stow Sunday School banner. (DG) CENTRE: South Kyme group, 1886, outside the barn they used as a Wesleyan chapel — and BELOW: at the opening of the new chapel the same day.

TO ALL MINISTERS AND LOCAL PREACHERS

Will you please SPEAK UP. You have a message: let the people hear it.

ABOVE: SPEAK UP notice to preachers. LEFT: Francis and Elizabeth Riggall of Dexthorpe. BELOW: Charles Richardson, the Lincolnshire Thrasher, and his cottage. (DNR)

LINCOLN

𝕴𝖊𝖘𝖑𝖊𝖞𝖆𝖓 𝕭𝖆𝖓𝖉 𝖔𝖋 𝕳𝖔𝖕𝖊,

ESTABLISHED Nov. 16th, 1855,

For the Promotion of Total Abstinence principles among the young, & for the advancement of Morality & Religion.

President.
Rev. M. RANDLES.

Treasurer.
Mr. F. CROWDER.

Secretary.
Mr. WM. W. RICHARDSON.

Mr. C. F. COTTAM, Assistant Secretary.

RULES FOR JUVENILE MEMBERS.

1. That the adoption of Total Abstinence principles and the maintenance of good moral conduct be essential to your membership.

2. Upon the approval of your parents to the following Declaration, "I AGREE TO ABSTAIN FROM ALL INTOXICATING DRINKS, AND FROM TOBACCO IN ALL ITS FORMS," your name shall be inscribed upon a Card of Membership, for which you shall pay the sum of one penny, and, upon your ceasing to be a Member, you shall return the said Card to the Secretary.

3. You will also be required to contribute one penny per month to the funds of the Society, to be paid the first Friday in each month. In return for this subscription you will receive a Ticket, to be renewed quarterly, which will admit you to the ordinary meetings of the Society. You will also be entitled to receive a copy of the Band of Hope Review, or the Adviser, each month, and a ticket for the Tea Meetings held in July and November; but no member can receive a ticket for either of the Tea Meetings before having been enrolled six months, without paying the difference between the amount of subscription and the price of the ticket.

4. Leave home in time to be at the place of meeting at five minutes before seven o'clock every Friday evening.

5. On entering the meeting proceed at once quietly to the seat assigned to you.

6. Do not leave it until the conclusion of the meeting, unless requested to do so by the Superintendent.

7. Avoid taking anything with you that would divert your attention from the lesson of the evening.

8. Endeavour to do everything required of you in the best manner you can ; for that which is worth doing, ought to be done well.

9. When singing, try how sweetly and correctly you can follow the leader.

10. During prayer, stand upright, keep off the forms, keep your eyes closed all the time, and let every word of the prayer be as from your own hearts.

11. Read attentively and preserve carefully all the books, tracts, hymns, or other things that you receive.

12. When you are alone, pray to God for the poor children whose parents use intoxicating liquors, that He may enable them to resist the temptations to which they are exposed.

13. Induce your companions to attend the meetings ; if you only get one each week, that will be fifty-two in a year.

14. These meetings are designed to make you acquainted with the dangerous nature of alcoholic drinks, tobacco snuff, and opium, that you may avoid them.

15. Those who manage them will, in a few years, be removed by death,—qualify yourself to carry them on when they are dead.

William Hayes, Printer, Lincoln.

ABOVE: Lincoln Wesleyan Band of Hope rules. BELOW: Local Preachers in Skegness Circuit at Mumby in the 1890s.

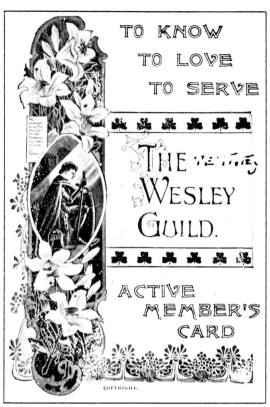

LEFT: Tetney Wesley Guild member's pledge card. BELOW: June Quarterly Meeting at Stainfield near Bourne, 1896. (DNR) RIGHT: Members gather at Saltfleetby St Peter for the stone laying of the P.M. chapel, opened 1907.

TRINITY WESLEYAN CHURCH.
STAMFORD.

OPENING OF NEW ORGAN.

Order of Services
AND

= RECITALS =

BY

H. KEETON, ESQ., Mus. Doc.
(Organist of Peterborough Cathedral)

AND

GATTY SELLARS, ESQ.,
OF LONDON,
(Solo Organist for Great Festival at the Crystal Palace, 1908.)

Artistes :

Miss DORIS MERRICK (Soprano),
(Queen's Hall, Etc.)

Miss GRETA HARDY (Mezzo-Soprano),
(Pupil of Madame Dewhurst.)

ANTHEMS BY THE CHOIR (AUGMENTED).

THURSDAY, JUNE 18th,
and
SUNDAY, JUNE 21st,
1908.

Price of this Programme Sixpence.

Trinity Wesleyan Church,
STAMFORD.

Preliminary Announcement
OF A

BAZAAR

Proposed to be held (D.V.) in the

Corn Exchange, Stamford,

OR

Monday, Tuesday, and Wednesday,

December 3rd, 4th, and 5th, 1888,

LEFT: Opening of new organ at Trinity Wesleyan, Stamford, 1908.
RIGHT: Stamford Trinity Wesleyan church Bazaar, 1888. BELOW: North
Somercotes Manse, built 1871. (DNR) OPPOSITE: Stamford Indian
Palace Bazaar, 1892.

" The love of variety seems woven into the frame of every son and daughter of Adam."—STERNE.

OFFICIAL HANDBOOK

OF THE GRAND

Indian Palace Bazaar

TO BE HELD IN THE

CORN EXCHANGE, STAMFORD,

ON

Monday, Tuesday, & Wednesday,

February 22nd, 23rd, & 24th, 1892.

TIMES OF OPENING.

☞ Monday at 2.30.   Admission 1s.

☞ Tuesday at 2.30.   Admission 6d.

☞ Wednesday at 2.30.   Admission 6d.

Children under 12 years half-price.

SEASON TICKET for the three days, 1s. 6d., to admit as often as desired.

TICKETS may be obtained at Mr. POTTER's (late Jenkinsons') High Street; Mr. H. HOBKIRK, High Street; Mr. T. D. PARRISH, High Street; Mr. J. DUNSTAN, High Street; Mr. A. D. JACKSON, Red Lion Square; Mr. H. T. DANIELS, All Saints' Place; Mr. A. DOBBS, Maiden Lane; Mr. E. BOWMAN, Bentley Street; Mr. H. HART, Broad Street; and others.

N.B.—-You cannot go in without paying, but you can pay without going in.

" To say you are welcome were superfluous."—SHAKESPEARE.

LEFT: Primitive Methodist Great Gathering ticket for Scotter. RIGHT: Grantham Wesleyan harvest festival, 1905. BELOW: Opening of Scotter Wesleyan chapel, 1900. (BL)

Multiplication by Division

Multiplication by division is the mathematical means of calculating the growth of Methodism. With about 4,000 members in 1800, a century later they numbered 33,600 in Lincolnshire. The national figure was over a million. Sunday school scholars were counted in the thousands. This growth is accounted for by a number of agencies.

The Primitive Methodists continued their camp meeting evangelism well into the present century. These big events were held in the open air and attracted hundreds of people. Market Rasen is a typical example. 'After addresses had been delivered to the idlers who frequent the market place, the people marched to the field . . . The speakers severally, in delivering their addresses [which included the religious and political] laboured hard to edify and instruct the hearers'. At Scotter the camp meeting was held on a Monday, but the way had been prepared on Sunday with four sermons, two in the chapel, one in the marquee and one on the village green. At 7 o'clock the next morning the meeting began, 'but as the day advanced it was cheering to the mind to see many and different vehicles enter the village. At one time near 2,000 people were on the ground listening to the gospel and between 800 and 900 took tea'.

Cheap trains were advertised at Barton upon Humber, from Hull and from Grimsby. When the South Yorkshire Railway opened a line in 1860 and placed a station near Crowle Wharf, expectation ran high for their annual camp meeting, 'nor were we disappointed'. It was Monday again and 'parties brought by train from Sheffield, Barnsley, Doncaster, Keadby . . . until thousands were collected'. The meetings lasted all day and yielded the sum of £60. There were thirty-five 'soul-stirring addresses'. By 1869 they added a new feature to the preaching — a bazaar. The motive was obviously to save souls and to make money!

Revival services were conducted in the chapels, usually lasting ten days, when some visiting evangelist was called in, all designed to bring the uncommitted to a decision. But increases in membership were not all the result of sporadic revivals, useful as these proved to be. The Wesleyans adopted a meeting known as the Wesley Guild, and other denominations had a meeting under the title Christian Endeavour. Both types were new and in some respects similar, and they became a modern alternative to the already declining class meeting, dating back to Wesley. The Guild had a broad outlook and included a literary and musical evening, while the Christian Endeavour was Bible based and chiefly devotional. Both required member involvement; people were called on to prepare a paper on a given topic, while the musical evening brought out the latent talent of those who could sing or play some musical instrument. This involvement was also a challenge, and many folk learned how to speak in public; from both the Guild and the Endeavour came new preachers and leaders.

The Mutual Improvement Society was an innovation of some of the town chapels, its name giving a clue to its aim. There was one at Wainfleet, where a programme shows that politics and literary subjects were debated. Both Wesley and Hannah Memorial in Lincoln had a Mutual Improvement Society and any syllabus reveals the wide variety of subjects considered during a winter session. This broader programme had similar results to those of the Guild, fostering interest and bringing out the talents of members, some of whom branched out into politics and social services. These had their counterpart in the more secular life of the towns, in the work done by the Mechanics' Institutes, the Workers' Educational Association, the Co-op Guilds and the like.

The class meeting was still significant in many places. They too had results far beyond the chapel where they met. Tom Hill's class at Hannah Memorial, Lincoln sent out many people into the wider connexion, some as ministers and missionaries, many as preachers and church officials.

The Methodists influenced other movements, for example the Agricultural Trade Unions, when a bid was made for better wages and farming conditions. The impetus came from preachers already gifted at speaking, but there were others whose talents lay in administration, and they became union officials. Some who engaged in these activities were disciplined by the Quarterly Meeting for taking part in union activities. Elial Harrison, for example, was disciplined for being 'largely involved with Labourers' Union', but he was not expelled, only admonished for 'an error of judgement'. The Methodists saw their involvement with the Union as a divine vocation, while others feared the possibility of violence, occasioned no doubt by the inflammatory outbursts in some speechers. Speaking at Deeping Fen, George Ball referred to the lords of creation who 'suck your blood and wear out your sinews to fill their own pockets . . . They have robbed you of roadside grass'. William Banks of Claypole was equally vitriolic: 'They can buy pianos for their daughters, they can keep governesses to educate them, and they themselves have bellies like sacks of wheat'. But there was no violence and, though the movement was shortlived, while it lasted it drew men together in a united effort to improve working conditions, and with good results. Most of the meetings were held in chapels, often they opened with prayer, and some of the speeches had Old Testament prophetic overtones.

Another agency of potential and practical increase was through the educational establishments set up by the Wesleyans — the day schools. There were over seventy in the county, most of them the result of a concern for social discipline and religious training. The teachers were drawn from the Methodist members, many of them preachers or leaders. There was a Methodist society at Kelstern Hall, the home of Roger Sharpley and, when a day school was set up in the hall, Christopher Ludlam became the headmaster. He had fought at Corunna and lost an arm while engaged with Wellington in the Peninsular War and when invalided out of the Army, became a preacher and teacher.

The Methodists engaged in other activities, both for the interest and the benefit of its members. Such were the 'Louth Methodist Funeral Brief Society', founded in 1855 and soon with a membership of 371. At Horncastle there was the Wesleyan Benefit Society, and at Grantham the Wesleyan Provident Society. In Gainsborough there was a Sick and Dividing Club run by the Primitive Methodists. Many Methodists were members of lodges of Oddfellows, Free Gardeners and Rechabites.

Individual Methodists used their gifts and influence in a variety of ways, believing that membership of a society required practical service to their fellow men. The Riggalls of Lincolnshire wielded great influence in the farming communities around Tetford and Ulceby. William Riggall employed Charles Richardson, who became known as the 'Lincolnshire Thrasher' and travelled the county as a freelance evangelist with remarkable results. Francis Riggall had a varied career, beginning life as a draper in Alford, then giving it up to become a tract distributor, travelling as far as Scotland and in Ireland on horseback. When he died, he left large sums of money to many Wesleyan institutions, as well as legacies for the poor at Alford and Louth.

The Thorold family of Harmston numbered among its members a bishop and several clergymen, but Benjamin, High Steward of Lincoln, was a Methodist preacher, who began the study of the Hebrew Bible at the age of seventy. Sir Robert Perks, Liberal MP for Louth (1892-1910) came of a Methodist background, his father being a Wesleyan Minister and, during his years of association with Louth, gave liberally to many chapels, presiding at the large gatherings and laying the foundation stones of a number of chapels. He inaugurated what was known as Twentieth Century Fund, sometimes called the Million Guineas Fund, a scheme he saw to its conclusion while he was at the height of his Parliamentary career.

Many of the towns, including Lincoln city, had Methodist Mayors and Councillors, as well as a large number of Justices of the Peace, people also prominent in the civic and business life of their own town. Alderman Henry Smethurst JP of Grimsby, son of a Primitive Methodist travelling preacher, became a preacher himself, and spent his whole life in civic affairs. He was trustee of nearly a score of chapels and at the forefront in the establishment of the Hainton Avenue and Flottergate chapels. Twice Mayor, chairman of the school board, and a prosperous businessman, he was the architect of his own fortunes, giving to all sorts of causes, and within two years of his death a marble monument to his memory was placed in the People's Park.

C.T. Parker was three times Mayor of Lincoln, and Joseph Broadberry rose from the working class to the city magisterial bench. Lincoln had a succession of Methodist Mayors in Hugh Wyatt, William Wallis, John W. Ruddock, Edward Harrison and Albert Hall. There was J.W. Morton of Louth, John Beulah, sixty-two years a preacher and three times Mayor of Boston, and Herbert Hart of Stamford. These were all either trustees of chapels or leaders, preachers or Sunday school teachers. One outstanding character in Lincoln was John R. Halkes, an architect by profession, often seen cycling in the city when he was over ninety years of age. He took up the collection at Wesley Chapel and usually told the preacher to speak up as he left the communion rail. His memorial is in a number of foundation stones of several chapels in and around Lincoln.

The county gave many men to the itinerant ministry, some of whom rose to high position in the Connexion. Amos Burnett of Little Steeping became a President, as did Joseph Bush of Ashby by Partney. Some went to the foreign field, as it was called in Victorian days: Aaron Edman, born at Bardney, went to the West Indies, and to the same field went George H.B. Hay, a Fotherby man. Jabez Langford, born at East Heckington, went to Australia, and William J.H. Picken of Lincoln to India. All the towns and many villages had sons in the ministry.

The less talented laymen were part of this Methodism too. Weaver Allison of Theddlethorpe wrote in his own inimitable style a journal which describes life in a village and a man's feelings and aspirations: 'What a blessing it is that I see another market day wherein I may trade and get gain for my soul. The Sabbath is like unto a large fair day where there is many valuable jewels to be given away to anyone who will accept them'. The chapel was the main thing in his life. John Thompson of Langworth, like Charles Richardson of Tetford, was an evangelist who moved around the county and kept a diary of events, all very simple, but most revealing.

The Victorians held grand bazaars to extinguish debts on their buildings. Stamford held one called the 'Grand Indian Palace Bazaar' covering three days, to raise what we might judge to be a modest sum of £300. The appeal was to help the final struggle to clear a debt and, besides the many stalls, there was entertainment by an orchestral band, marionettes and a ventriloquist.

There were special meetings in the town chapels to bring together the whole circuit, when the President of the Conference came, or some other giant preacher from the provinces, and there was stirring singing, the more uplifting because the grand organ and choir gave a magnificent lead. The large chapels became centres for fine music in great variety: cantatas and oratorios and anthems on special occasions. One notable choirmaster, who had a tablet to his memory in Wainfleet chapel, was Alfred Rogerson, who conducted the Choral Society and compiled a collection of old Methodist tunes as a centenary volume to mark the anniversary of the death of Wesley.

Anniversaries were occasions for much singing and tea meetings. At Market Rasen it was reported that 'the tables were decorated with every variety of choice flowers, and groaned under the weight of viands, sufficient to satisfy the appetite of the most fantastic epicure'. There were fraternal exchanges between villages, Sunday school anniversaries, harvest festivals, family gatherings at christenings and funerals.

There was a growing awareness of the need for a wider social outreach. The Flottergate Benevolent Committee started with a legacy of £2,852 bequeathed by a Miss Atkin and, under the influence of such men as Captain Sir William Edge MP and Alderman James Blindell MP, nine Methodist homes were built for poorer people. Special funds were inaugurated to meet emergency needs, and local chapels gave support to national institutions, such as Dr Barnado's, the National Children's Homes, or some remote, yet urgent, appeal for disasters in the mines or at sea.

The annual Missionary meeting was a feature of all the chapels, and to have a 'live' missionary present was to give the meeting a reality. Henry Lunn, a Horncastle man, went as a missionary to India with a degree in medicine and, when he was forced to leave India, he wrote regularly in the *Methodist Times* on missionary policy, at the same time giving himself to the business of providing lawn tennis equipment. Others had gone overseas and came home to tell a lively tale, and by it inspired much giving to the missionary cause. There was large generosity also to the city missions, who were working for the poor in many a slum area.

There was expansion in what were called the watering places, when the Victorians first discovered the simple joys of a holiday at Cleethorpes, Mablethorpe or Skegness, and these once remote villages became lively centres of Methodist activity. Away from the coast, Scunthorpe, with its group of villages, grew to an enormous conurbation, and the Methodists scattered chapels across the whole township, benefitting by the boom in the steel industry.

Methodist documents range from the private diary to minute books and preaching plans, all part of the increasing wealth of a movement which makes up the life of the people and the activities in the chapels. Richard Cook lived at South Ferriby and tells in his journal of people he knew. John Gibson was 'a useful man in the Wesleyan chapel who started all the tunes'. William Fellowes, known as Shooter Willie, had a large duck gun and a small shooting boat, shot 21 wild ducks all at one go and, on the following Sunday, 'thanked the great Father of all for his good fortune'. William Dawson, a butcher and preacher, entertained people with stories of Alma, Inkerman and Balaclava, and Dicky Skinner, famous for long sermons, on entering the pulpit was cautioned by the farm lads; 'Now Dicky remember what day thou goes on'.

John Smith of Lincoln left his diary, in which he tells much of business life but more of events in the chapels. The diary of John Cussons, baker at Horncastle, fifty years a preacher, was introspective in many parts: 'very much cast down', 'worse than ever', 'not much feeling', 'pretty good', were comments as he reflected on his Sunday efforts.

But the preaching plan had and still has its own distinctive place in Methodism, and local plans reveal the characteristics of the Ministers who made them. One at Market Rasen advised: 'It would be well, perhaps to affix it to the wall in some conspicuous part of the house, or attach it securely to the family Bible'. The Gainsborough Superintendent reminded his preachers that he who 'neglects his appointments must assign his reason for such neglect to the Quarterly Meeting . . . and if his reason is not satisfactory, his name shall be absolutely taken off the plan'. Such was the discipline. Some Ministers used space to provide verse, such as Thomas Cocking at Grantham who wrote:

'Again the plan presents itself to view   'Tis at they service, and its price is small,
   Its use is ancient, though its date is new;   That plans are useful is allowed by all.

The minute books tell more, for both styles of reporting and matters discussed, and along with financial statements reveal our Victorian forebears as loyal, perhaps in some instances eccentric, yet all devoted to the societies and circuits throughout the county. When Queen Victoria died, the Methodists were on the crest of the wave.

WESLEYAN-METHODIST
LOCAL PREACHERS' MUTUAL AID
ASSOCIATION.

ON SUNDAY JULY 8TH, 1888,

SERMONS ON BEHALF OF THE ABOVE WILL BE PREACHED AS FOLLOWS:—

BAILGATE WESLEYAN CHAPEL,

10.30,
MR. A. R. JOHNSON
Of NOTTINGHAM.

6.0,
MR. M. ATKINSON,
Of LEEDS.

WESLEY CHAPEL, CLASKET GATE,

10.30,
MR. M. ATKINSON,
Of LEEDS.

6.0,
MR. A. R. JOHNSON,
Of NOTTINGHAM.

SILVER STREET FREE METHODIST CHAPEL,

10.30,
CAPTAIN KING,
Of CLAPTON.

6.0,
Mr. M. L. CLAPHAM,
Of BAYSWATER.

HIGH STREET WESLEYAN CHAPEL,

10.30,
MR. CANDLER,
Of BRIXTON HILL.

6.0,
MR. AMPHLETT,
Of OXFORD.

PORTLAND STREET FREE METHODIST CHAPEL,

10.30,
Mr. M. L. Clapham
Of BAYSWATER.

6.0,
Captain KING,
Of CLAPTON.

ST. CATHERINE'S WESLEYAN CHAPEL,

10.30,
Mr. Amphlett
Of OXFORD.

6.0,
Mr. Candler,
Of BRIXTON HILL.

ON MONDAY, JULY 9TH,
A PUBLIC MEETING
Will be held in WESLEY CHAPEL,

When Addresses will be given by Ministers of the City, the above-named Gentlemen and other Friends.

CHAIR TO BE TAKEN AT 7.30, BY JOHN SMITH, ESQ., J.P.

COLLECTION AT ALL THE SERVICES IN AID OF THE ASSOCIATION'S FUNDS.

William Hayes, Steam Printer and Stationer, 46, Melville Street, Lincoln.

Local Preachers' Mutual Aid meeting, Lincoln, 1888.

ABOVE LEFT: Rev Thomas Overton who lived to be 102 (1833-1935).
(DNR) RIGHT: Billingborough Sunday School and banner, c1930. (DNR)
BELOW LEFT: Wesleyan Circuit Choir Festival, Market Rasen, 1906.
RIGHT: Wesleyan Conference, Lincoln, 1909 — Seamen's Mission
meeting.

MARKET RASEN

= Wesleyan Church. =

Annual Circuit

CHOIR FESTIVAL

Thursday, October 25th, 1906.

Tea in the Schoolroom at 5 o'clock, 9d.

Coffee Supper, 6d.

Grand Musical Service

At 6-30.

Soprano Soloist—
MADAME HANDLEY SMITH (Grimsby).
Organist—MR. J DUFFELL, Mus. Bac.
Chairman—MR. C. FIELDSEND.
Speaker—REV. W. HOAD.
Conductor—MR. H. PAYNE.

N.B. This Programme admits the Member
to Supper, free of charge.

H. PAYNE, PRINTER, MARKET RASEN.

WESLEYAN CONFERENCE,

LINCOLN, 1909.

Superintendent & Secretary:
REV. DAVID ROE,
QUEEN VICTORIA SEAMEN'S REST,
POPLAR, E.

On Monday, July 26th, at 7.30 p.m.
A MEETING

ON BEHALF OF THE

SEAMEN'S MISSION

WILL BE HELD IN THE
WESLEYAN CHURCH, LOUTH.

SPEAKERS:
Rev. JAMES D. LAMONT (Of BELFAST, Ex-President of the Irish Conference.)
Rev. JOHN H. GOODMAN   Rev. JOHN BELL
Rev. JOHN GAWTHROP   Rev. DAVID ROE
and others.
Chairman - Sir ROBERT W. PERKS, Bart., M.P.

Special Hymn Sheets provided. Special Music and Singing by the
Choir, under the direction of the Organist.
Soloist - Madame JESSIE STRATHEARN.
COLLECTION FOR SEAMEN'S MISSION.

ABOVE: Little Hale Sunday School Anniversary, 19 May 1914. BELOW:
Billinghay Band of Hope choir, 1909. (HJ) OPPOSITE ABOVE:
Scredington Sunday School outing, 1909. (Both DNR) BELOW: Wesleyan
chapel, Holland Fen. (DNR)

LEFT: Sir Henry Lunn of Horncastle, who gave £1,000 to the Missionary Society in 1925. (DNR) ABOVE: Opening of Searby chapel, 1909. BELOW: Haven Bank Sunday School outing to Skegness, 1929. (HL)

ABOVE: Haven Bank old chapel, 1935 — and BELOW: opening of the new chapel, 1936. (Both HL)

ABOVE: A group of Primitive Methodists at Horncastle, 1911. (DNR)
BELOW: Wesleyan Home Mission Gospel Car. (DNR)

ABOVE: Horncastle Wesleyan Tea party, 1920s. (DNR)
BELOW: Horncastle Wesleyan Sunday School Treat, 1921.
(DNR)

ABOVE: Singing Anniversary hymns round the villages, 1935. (DNR)
BELOW: School treat at Fulletby. (DNR)

OPPOSITE ABOVE: Goulceby Sunday School outing, 1909. (HS) CENTRE: Ropsley Sunday School anniversary, 1926. (DNR) BELOW: Louth Wesleyan Sunday School outing, 1900. (DNR) LEFT: Jesse Hall, Louth organist. (DNR) RIGHT: John Cussons, Horncastle miller and Local Preacher. (LEC) CENTRE: Dorrington Sunday School and chapel, 1908. (DNR)

ABOVE: Waltham Sunday School outing to Cleethorpes, 4 August 1914.
(DNR) BELOW: Stone laying of Scunthorpe Trinity Wesleyan chapel,
August 1898. (DNR)

LEFT: James Blindell, MP for Boston with Holland. (DNR) RIGHT: Sir
Robert Perks, MP for Louth. BELOW: Twentieth century Fund Certificate.
(OT)

LEFT: Twentieth century Fund pulpit in Louth 'Centenary' chapel. (DNR)
RIGHT: Louth 'Centenary' organ with T.L. Jubbs at the console and W.H. Jubbs voicing the pipes, 1924. (HJ) CENTRE: Bowthorpe Oak, near Bourne, England's largest girthed tree. For Bourne Wesleyan Sunday School treat 39 people crowded in and later 13 sat down for tea. (DNR)
BELOW: Temperance Demonstration at the Priory in Louth, June 1916.

Union

The Methodists were all united in 1932. A union in 1907 between some of the sections passed almost unnoticed in Lincolnshire, but it prepared the way for the fuller union. Since the days of John Wesley, Methodists have counted their members. Attendances, always larger than the number of committed members, have only been estimated, but proved by analysis to be about three times greater. The Ecclesiastical Census of 1851 was a government exercise, not a Methodist one, and this revealed the numbers actually attending chapels and churches. The strength and weakness of Methodism has been measured generally by the increase or decrease of committed members. 1932 was statistically a disaster.

There were 27,300 members in 1932 in 64 Circuits and served by 93 Ministers. Fifty years later the members were reduced to 13,247 in 25 Circuits with 53 Ministers. Chapels were reduced from over 1,000 to about 350 in the same period.

The signing of the Deed of Union in the Albert Hall, London, on 20 September 1932 marked the end of the divisions and the beginning of a new era for the Methodist Church. The immediate task was consolidation, amalgamation and dealing with redundant chapels. Amalgamation of some circuits was easy, and quickly adopted, whilst others were more complicated. Louth, for instance, comprised 72 separate societies in three circuits, but with remarkable rapidity much was resolved. Where there were three chapels in a village, one served the whole and two were sold. That was true throughout the county.

While redundancy was dealt with, at the same time new enterprises arose. The new Central Hall in Grimsby was opened in 1936, an imaginative scheme which brought together several chapels in the Duncombe Street area. In other places old chapels gave way to new ones, in most cases in new areas, for instance Boston Zion, Grimsby Laceby Road, St Giles in Lincoln, and the Godfrey Memorial at Saxilby.

During the 1950s there were signs of growth. The age of the galleried chapel was over. The big Victorian structures gave way to new all-purpose buildings in the suburbs of most towns. There was an upsurge in membership in the period of Macmillan's assertion 'you have never had it so good'. But it was a temporary 'good'. If the 1960s and 1970s saw the decline of members and preachers, they also saw the streamlining of Methodism throughout the land. A new generation built chapels suited to new purposes, while the people themselves experimented with new types of worship.

Conversations on Anglican-Methodist unit, hopefully started, ended in the 1970s in frustration and failure, but ecumenical ventures grew, exemplified in joint house groups, more frequent ecumenical services, and combined discussions on community projects. The Bishop of Grimsby opened a new church in Gainsborough and the Bishop of Lincoln was quite frequently speaking at Methodist services, while clergymen assisted at some chapel openings, and their names began to appear on Methodist preaching plans.

But Methodism maintained its characteristic style in many places. Born in song, as the historian is keen to remind us, singing was still the predominant characteristic of many occasions.

There was no instrument to lead the singing at Spalding Crescent for a long period, but Mr Brett led with the aid of a tuning fork. Harry Carradice of Woodhall led the singing with a violin, continued to use it after the organ was installed, while a man at Dunholme led with his cornet. The purchase of a harmonium was a great event in the life of the village chapel, but it was the great organ in the town chapel which provided the music, and the introduction of choirs made for many a grand occasion.

There were many capable organists serving the town churches over a long period. In Grimsby there were A.C.Storr, Sydney Grice and Percy Wilson, C.R.Jones at Cleethorpes, J.R.Bee and C.W.Page at Lincoln, Jesse Hall, the blind organist at Louth and the Bennetts in the same town, and Wilfred Allen in Grantham. The Grimsby Central Hall was renowned for its musical events in great variety, when the Philharmonic Choir under Alec Redshaw gave *Messiah* with leading soloists such as Isabel Baillie, Kathleen Ferrier, Heddle Nash, Owen Brannigan and locally born Norma Proctor. Grimsby Flottergate choir under E.R.Benton presented such works as *Hiawatha*, *Carmen* and *Merrie England*, and the choir at Roman Bank, Skegness performed Bach's *St Matthew Passion*.

'A feast of music' was a newspaper heading of an event at Market Rasen, when the chapel 'was filled to overflowing, the occasion being the eighth annual choir festival'. Smaller chapels had their musical treats! East Halton gathered a choir capable of performing *Messiah*, while a group of villages around Willingham by Stow formed themselves into a modest but well-received 'Sankey Choir'.

The magic lantern had its useful part to play in both entertainment and in education for, as a visual aid, it taught young people the work on the mission field or the tragic scenes of London's poor. The film projector was its successor in bringing the Bible before people in dramatic form. These forerunners of television were widely used in chapels and Sunday schools and among the young.

In 1944 the Methodist Association of Youth Clubs was born, a powerfully organised drive to capture young people in the atmosphere of church life. This more than any other agency became the major attraction in the post-war years. St Catherines in Lincoln was in many ways a pioneer, inaugurated by Philip Race, achieving national fame with an imaginative programme, emulated by many far and wide. But not all the activity of the youth clubs was merely to meet the needs of those wanting either entertainment or a place to develop other skills, though these were the aims of most. Bracebridge Youth Club looked outwardly and set themselves to raise money for guide dogs for the blind, bulls for India and the leprosy mission. Across the county, many villages had their clubs, and success marked many of those, despite recession, replaced in some instances by the more charismatic approach where young people began to discover new forms of worship and religious expression.

The Methodist Conference never met in Lincolnshire after 1932, but in earlier years the Wesleyans had met in Lincoln, while the Primitive Methodists met five times in Grimsby, and the United Free Methodists three times in Louth. These conferences brought the wider connexion to the doors of local people and were stirring events, particularly in such services as ordination of Ministers and public rallies.

Lincolnshire produced a few Presidents: Richard Watson, John Hannah, Amos Burnett, Joseph Bush, John Beecham, William C. Jackson, William E. Farndale, Henry Bett and John A. Newton. Lincoln city produced one Vice-President in Philip H. Race.

The Aggregate meeting of the Local Preachers Mutual Aid Association met three times in Lincoln and twice in Louth, and several preachers in the county were among its Presidents. The Association opened a Home for retired preachers at Woodhall Spa and, by the inspiration of Philip Race, a Methodist Home for the Aged was opened by the Duchess of Kent in 1972 at Stones Place, Lincoln.

Worship patterns changed in many chapels, using such groups as Mission Bands and developing the Family Service. Congregations more and more preferred the morning service to the evening, which became the pattern in the last decade or two. New members were recruited from within after receiving a course of training, and new forms of weekday events catered for modern needs, such as pram and pushchair service, the young wives' groups, and house meetings. The time-honoured women's meeting continues to the present day, having a secure place alongside the Anglican Mothers' Union; the two often join as one.

Nor is the generation of preachers extinct and many, like the three former divisions of the county, still preach a three-fold sermon. To the discerning eye there is much in the county which is nostalgic of former days, for a few chapels remain which remind one of the Victorians and, if some modern form of heating has replaced the old combustion stove, there is in many of the chapels a warmth characteristic of the days when Methodists met in their own dwellings and worked hard to erect a chapel. The hard work of recent days is in restoring some of the hundred year old fabric, and attempting to beautify the place still known as 'the Chapel'.

Lincolnshire Methodism continues to play a vital role in the life of every town and in many villages. What has been related here of the history of the movement is a continuing evolution in the lives of many people who serve the church, and who play an important part in the community, in many organisations and in remedial services, where they live and work.

RIGHT: A. C. Storr, organist at George Street, Grimsby. (DNR)
BELOW: Grimsby Flottergate choir, 1930. (DNR)

121

ABOVE: Louth Eastgate Pantomime which ended on the night of the East Coast Floods, 31 January 1953. (BR) BELOW: Opening of the Link Chapel at Louth in 1960. Miss Elizabeth Sharpley with the Rev Horace Marshall (centre) and Canon Ward, Rector of Louth (right).

LEFT: Stone laying of Monks Road chapel, Lincoln, 1961 by John R. Halkes. BELOW: Stone laying of West Parade school hall, Lincoln, 1962 by C.E. Empringham, with the author extreme left. RIGHT: Wilfred Allen, organist at Finkin Street, Grantham for 50 years and still playing. (GJ)

ABOVE: Horncastle Queen Street Young Men's Brotherhood, 1932. (DNR) BELOW: Tea meeting at Bullington in the 1960s, with Rev Fred Bond.

LEFT: Dr. Henry Bett, born at Maidenwell in the Wolds, President of the Conference, 1940. RIGHT: Philip H. Race of Lincoln, Vice President of the Conference, 1957. (PHR)

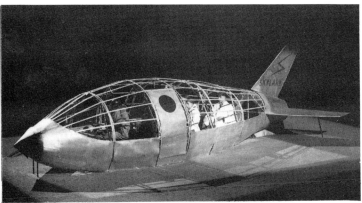

St Marks, Scunthorpe, 1962, INSET: St Catherines, Lincoln display at the Methodist Association of Youth Clubs in the Royal Albert Hall, London, 1953. (PHR)

ABOVE: Birchwood, Lincoln, 1966. CENTRE: East Halton, 1967.
BELOW: Harrowby Lane, Grantham, 1963.

The Uniting Conference of the Methodist Church, London, September
1932.

Wesley Celebrations

MAY 24th 1738

LINCOLN 1988

Post Script

by Rev Alan J. Davies MA

This book has been published to coincide with the celebrations of the 250th anniversary of John Wesley's Aldersgate experience on 24 May 1738. It is particularly appropriate that William Leary has written about another Lincolnshire man and the results of his experience as evidenced by the story of Methodism in our country, and 1988 is indeed a special milestone.

However, it is a milestone rather than a destination. Sometime in the distant future I hope there will be *Volume II* which tells the story after 1988. What will that story be? Will it have a definite end, when Methodism will have completed her task and become part of a united Church in England? The fact that the climax of our Lincolnshire Methodist celebrations will be in Lincoln Cathedral, in the presence of all our sister churches, is itself a symbol of the new spirit of friendship and co-operation. Having been involved in previous abortive efforts to unite the churches, I have no illusion about the difficulties which lie ahead if this is to be the end of the story, but personally still hope and pray that it is a destination I will live to see.

In the meantime there will be exciting stories to tell. Many of us are beginning to realise how important are the changes taking place in Lincolnshire, as the fifth county in England in the table of population growth. In meeting those changes as we become part of the new commuter belt, receive those involved in the high technology industries, develop our historic and scenic heritage for those at leisure or in retirement, and adapting our agriculture and land use for the twenty-first century, I believe that Methodism has an important part to play. Its peculiar heritage has been to hold together the need for individual religious experience, and involvement in the community of village, farm, city and nation. As we try to look at the future for Lincolnshire it seems clear that this task for the Methodist people will be as important in the next century as in the last 250 years, whether within a larger church or continuing the present pattern of co-operation. And in so doing we shall be immensely helped by this first volume and the history it contains.

Bibliography

Baker, Frank *The Story of Cleethorpes* (1953)

Birtwhistle, Allen *In His Armour. The Life of John Hunt of Fiji* (1954)

Clarke, J.N. & Anderson C.L. *Methodism in the Countryside: Horncastle Circuit 1786—1986*

Coulson, J.E. *The Peasant Preacher. Memorials of Charles Richardson* (1867)

Cocking, Thomas *The History of Wesleyan Methodism in Grantham and its Vicinity* (1836)

Edwards, W. Le Cato *The Home of the Wesleys* (nd)

Hocken, Joshua *A Brief History of Wesleyan Methodism in the Grimsby Circuit* (1839)

Kendall, H.B. *The Origin and History of the Primitive Methodist Church* (c1906)

Leary, William *Methodism in the City of Lincoln* (1969)

   Methodism in the Town of Boston (1972)

   Wesley Chapel and Rosemary Lane Day Schools (1961)

Leary, W. & Robinson, David *A History of Methodism in Louth* (1981)

Lester, George *Grimsby Methodism and the Wesleys in Lincolnshire* (1890)

Robinson, P.W. 'Louth and the Rise of Free Methodism' *Journ. Lincs. Methodist History Society* (1977)

Russell, Rex *A History of Schools and Education in Lindsey 1800—1902* (1965)

   The 'Revolt of the Field' in Lincolnshire (1956)

Scotland, N.A.D. *Methodism and the Origin and Development of Agricultural Trade Unions in Lincolnshire 1872—96* (nd)

Shaw, George *Life of Parkinson Milson* (1893)

Sneath, H.A. *Methodist Memories* (Bourne, 1923)

Watmough, Abraham *Methodism in Lincoln* (1828)

White, M.G. '50 years of Re-United Methodism: some aspects of Lincolnshire Methodism 1932—82' *Journ. Lincs.*
   Methodist History Society (1986)

The Journal of John Wesley. Standard Edition. (8 vols) 1909

The Letters of John Wesley. Standard Edition. (8 vols) 1931

Lives of the Early Methodist Preachers. Edited by Thomas Jackson. 1865

Wesleyan Methodist Magazines 1778—1932

Primitive Methodist Magazines 1812—1932

United Methodist Free Churches Magazines 1857—1932

Methodist New Connexion Magazines 1797—1932

Minutes of the Methodist Conferences.

Centenary of the Methodist New Connexion Edited. 1897

Lincolnshire Directories 1856 & 1893

Diaries of John Smith, Weaver Allison, John Thompson, Richard Abey, Richard Cook.

Dissenting Certificates.

Local brochures on chapel Jubilees, &c.

Minute books, account books, schedule books, class books, &c.

Subscribers

Presentation Copies

1 The Old Rectory, Epworth
2 The Methodist Church, Westminster
3 Dr William Davies
4 Rev Dr John A. Newton
5 Rev Dr John A. Harrod MA, BSc
6 Rev Alan J. Davies MA

7 William Leary BA
8 David N. Robinson
9 Clive & Carolyn Birch
10 Mrs Nora Jones
11 Malcolm Darby
12 J. Bates
13 Brenda M. Laviolette
14 D. Colin Dews
15 Mrs Jean Sutton
16 Margaret Empson
17 Miss M.D. Rostron
18 Rev H. Snowden
     Enderby
19 Rev Ivor Haythorne
20 Peter Turner
21 John Fitchett
22 Mrs M.E. Lyon
23 G. Clayton
24 Mrs E.H. Mumby
25 Rev W. Motson
26 A.S. Turner
27 Richard Hollingsworth
28
30 Mrs M. Shaw
31 Bryan R. Utteridge
32 Geoffrey L. Holmes
33 Mrs G.M. Hicks
34 A.J. Light
35 Rex C. Russell
36 J.W. Belsham
37 David S. Wharton
38 Eric Sutcliffe
39 P.A. Pelham
40 Mrs P.A. Webster
41 Mrs E. Pickering
42 Cyril Todd
43 J.A. Hastings
44 T.W. Wilkinson
45 D. Burniston
46 Ernest Rawding
47 Harold Roberts
48 F.C. Pollard
49 Brian Russell Bailey
50 Mrs M. Leary
51 Enid H. Pittwood
52 Mrs D.S. Lynaugh
53 A. Rodgers

54 Rev Alan M. Barker
55 Mrs Florence R. Graves
56 R.G. Briggs
57 Arthur Dennis Baker
58 John Anthony Davies
59 Peter W. Robinson
60 Mrs Mary Collingwood
61 Pauline M. Gibson
62 B. Dickinson
63 H.B. Peaker
64 Brian Wass
65 Peter Cook
66 Mrs Eleanor Bennett
67 F.S. Peck
68 A.J. Atkinson
69 Dennis Gilbert
70 Mrs D. Bryant
71 Michael L. Coates
72 Jeffrey Hird
73 Mrs J. Sweeting
74 Mrs P. Hollingworth
75 Mr & Mrs D. Lowe
76 Rev John E. Minor MA
77 M. Jordan
78 R.S. Smith
79 Philip J. Mallinder
80 A. Campbell
81 Mrs P. Wooding
82 K.W. Sidebotham
83 David Cuppleditch
84 Mrs Katherine Adams
85 Gwyneth Owen
86 Harold Jackson
87 R.B. & J. Howard
88 Mrs P.H. Staunton
89 Mrs Joy McNish
90 Michael & Diana
     Honeybone
91 Laurence Elvin FSA
92 Philip Race
93 Iris E. Covell
94 Grace Dodsworth
95 Percy Panting
96 Christopher Stell
97 Dorothy Kingsbury
98 Lincolnshire
     Recreational
     Services

99 R. Bellamy
100 Lincolnshire Archives
      Office
101 John Richard Barker
102 Rev Arnold Skelding
103 Sarah E. Drury
104 Rev J. Neil Graham
105 C.P.C. Johnson
106 Colin Henry Clayton
107 W.P. Fotheringham
108
109 Mrs Beverley Ash
110 Epworth County
      Primary School
111 Claire Beisty
112 Walter Powdrill
113 K. Morley
114 P. Gregory
115 Mrs E. Batcheler
116 North Axholme
      Comprehensive
      School
117 Peter Hargreaves
118 Alan Stubbs
119 Miss M. Roberts
120 Alan James Worton
121 Nicholas Page
122 Frederick Coulam
123 Frederick Panton
124 Harold C. Panton
125 E.V Wray
126 Mrs E.J. Ekins
127 Mr & Mrs G. Bulmer-
      Kirby
128 Mrs E.M. Brieant
129 Mrs J.F. Hornsby
130 Mrs V.A. Wheatley
131 Malcolm G. Knapp
132 Clifford Dack
133
134 R.G. Tinkler
135 Hugh Brammer
136 Jose Percival
137 Mrs Judith Derby
138 Richard Johnson
139 Dr & Mrs M. Hewitson
140 J. Fenton

141 Mrs M.P. Lyth
142 Joyce G. Barker
143 M.P. Beech
144 Rev Ross Fowkes
145 Miss J. Peck
146 George Hall
147 Colin Gerald Fletcher
148 Miss A. Whittaker
149 Kay Edgar
150 Peter D. Gill
151 John M. Gill
152 R. & M. Drummond
153 Margaret Gaunt
154 Mrs B.E. Blee
155 Mrs E.L. Fox
156 Mrs E.I. Bailey
157 Mrs S.C. Shaw
158 Mrs Hazel M. Lawson
159 Derek Warner
160 Neil & Marian Hatfield
161 F.H. Pearson
162 John V. Skellern
163
164 Monica Smith
165 Mr & Mrs J.D. Haden
166 J.B. Marriott
167
168 David George Norris
169 Rev Alan J. Davies
170 Mr & Mrs D. Brydges
171 William Bluck
172 Philip Walden
173 Kenneth Shelton Green
174 Mrs M.M. Theobald
175 Fred & Barbara Gill
176 Rev Albert Holland
177 John C.R. Stone
178 W.A. Rylatt
179 Colin Merrick
180 William Eric Haigh
181 John A. Vickers
182 Keith R. Guyler
183 Cyril J. Skinner
184
185 George Baines
186 John Sharples
187 Rev D.C. Kellington
188 T.S.A. Macquiban
189 Mrs Margaret Tomkiss
190 Stanley Young
191 C.T. Mackinder
192 Christopher Stark
193 Miss H. Sanderson
194 Jean Walsingham
195 Mrs G.V. Hickox
196 Robin Ward
197 Rosemary Oliver
198 H. Leary
199 Harry Goodwin
200 Joseph Neilson
201 James W. Richardson
202 Mrs Beryl Edwards
203 Mike & Mo Fricke
204 J. Turner
205 F.V. Brewster

206 William R. Cartledge
207 Mrs M. Nunn
208 Mrs M.J. Evans
209 J. Bradley
210 P.R. Spooner
211 Norman Douglas
212 H.C. Browne
213 G. Fred Lawe
214 Gwen & Maurice Haire
215 Fred Leary
216 J.G. Horner
217 Mrs E. Nicholls
218 Mrs N. Darrington
219 C.L. Anderson
220 N.J.L. Lyons
221 Mrs M. Wilson
222 Mr & Mrs S.C. Bell
223 Mrs M.E. Potts
224 John W. Holmes
225 Miss Ruth Tinley
226 Mrs Gracie Lawson
227 Miss B. Grantham
228 Enid Richardson
229 Mrs Annie Margaret
      Du Feu
230 Marcia Ivatt
231 Miss Mary Dixie
232 David Hicken
233 Eleanor Nannestad
234 J.R. Lainé
235 Mrs M.K. Whibley
236 Mrs D. Ballard
237 A. Roberts
238 John H. Edgington
239 Jennifer Margaret
      Thompson
240 Terence R. Leach
241 Norman Leveritt
242 David Leese
243 Mrs J.M. Priestley
244 Lincoln Theological
      College
245 Mrs J.M. Head
246 Frank Mosey
247 Dr R.W. Ambler
248 Dr & Mrs John B.
      Manterfield
249
250 Ken Redmore
251 Rev K.B. Renouf
252 Robert Land
253 Muriel Jean Hobbs
254 Nicola Holmes
255 Margaret Ellis
256 Mrs S.V. Hydes
257 David Kaye
258 Mrs Jill Makinson-
      Sanders
259 J.M. Proctor
260 R.W. Dales
261 W.O. Overton
262 Joan Cooling
263 Miss Elizabeth Hill
264 C.F. Markham
265
266 Margaret A. French

267 H.J.Faulkner
268 Winston Kime
269
270 John K. Marfleet
271 David H. Rees
272 Dr Williams's Library,
      London
273 Vicki Makin
274 G.E. & B.E. Smalley
275 Lucy Eileen Cussons
276 J. Norman Clarke
277 Doreen Palmer
278 Mr & Mrs W.R. Martin
279 Dorothy King
280
282 George A. Kastler
283 Mutual Aid Homes
284 F.T. Baker OBE
285 Rev J. Goodridge
286 Rev M.J. Logan
287 Mrs J.M. Parkin
288 Brenda Kelley
289 Rev Keith Howe
290 Miss P. Bossingham
291 R.R. Bradshaw
292 Charles Ekberg
293 David Cappitt
294 Greta Stratford
295 Eric Freeston
296 Eric Coxon
297 Mrs J. Pridgeon
298 M.H. Crosby
299 A.G. Bell
300 W. Mason Osbourne
301 Helen Ash
302 John Thomas Tait
303 John R. White
304 Grantham Journal
305 Mrs S.D. Roberts
306 Rev W. Eric Jones
307 Miss Beryl Cooling
308 B.E. Wilson
309 Frank Cammack
310 N. Dennis Corden
311 Mrs Joy Joy
312 Mr & Mrs G.L.
      Stephenson
313 J.G. Freeman
314 Rev David F. Hinson
315 Mrs Elsie Brown
316 Guy Anthony Elliott
317 Mrs Kathleen
      Stephenson
318 Miss Margaret
      Widdowson
319 Joan A. Grocock
320 Jennifer Rotton
321 Richard Hall
322 Philip Macdonald
323 Raymond Tinkler
324 Rev Dr O.A.
      Beckerlegge
325 Allan G. Griffin
326 J.W. Hollingworth
327 F. Crowder

328 A.J.L. Rogers
329 Frank Baker
330 C.M. Hardy
331 Martin Hodgkinson
332 Peter J. Shaw
333 F R. Sinderson
334 Mrs R.M. Yewdall
335 Scopwick
337 Methodist Church
338 Lincoln Cathedral
    Library
339 Barbara E. Lidgett
340 Bernice Stafford
341 Huibert & Judith M.
    van Oosterom
342 Mr & Mrs Felstead
343 Vivienne Draper
344 Cecil Jackson
345 Ted & Peg Hallett
346 Lincolnshire
368 Library Service
369 Rodney & Marlene
    Keightley
370 Mrs F. Blake
371 C.R. Wilkinson
372 J.S. English
373 Michael Hammond
374 F. Hill
375 Donald Owen
376
377 John Morgan
378 W. Miller
379 Rev Colin Membery
380 W.J.S. Quick
381 Hilda J. Thompson
382 C. Grimmer
383
384 Brian Gough
385 Michael D. Matsell
386 N.C. Cooke
387 Robert H. Brocklehurst
388 Alfred H. Wheatley
389 Mrs Margaret Houtby
390 Rev Eric W. Dykes
391 Michael Wardlow
392 Professor J.M. Rowson
393 Mrs Kathleen Fisher
394 Roy Clark
395
396 Ann M. Haith
397 Barry & Hilary Sutcliffe
398 Nellie Guy
399 Michael R. Stevens
400 J. Ingoldby
401 Mrs P.D. Carr
402 B.T. Stephens
403 J.M. Goodacre
404 Ms S. Cohen

405 David R. Hull
406 Barry R. Tointon
407 T. Norman Silson
408 Linda Crust
409 B. & E.R. Chappell
410 Joan Hewson
411 Paul R. Simpson
412 A.E.B. Fox
413 Jacqueline Ann Cecilia
    Sergeant
414 C.W. Craggs
415 Dr Clive D. Field
416 Anthony Kirk
417 Miss N. Kemble
418 David Parish
419 Vera North
420 D.A. Bellamy
421 Kevin M. Hart
422 Harold Jubbs
423 Miss N. Kemble
424 Rev G.L. Towell
425 Donald Harper
426 G. Houlden
427 Mrs E.M. Fenton
428 William Hugh Green
429 Mrs Croft
430 R. Dennis
431 Bernard Atkin
432
434 R.C. Reid
435 Olive Fytche
436 Venerable David
    Leaning
437 David H. Rees
438 Mrs J.P. Chamberlain
439 Mrs R.P. James
440 Mary Jordan
441
442 Godfrey Holmes
443 H.F. Bryant
444 K. Blow
445 Frank M. Amery
446 Mrs C. Robinson
447 A.J. Hawkins
448 Mrs A. Day
449 D. Aisthorpe
450 Pamela A. Crisp Beard
451 Mr & Mrs A. Dowling
452 G. Bartholomew
453 Alan Fairfield
454 Deirdre & Derek
    Holmes
455
456 Miss C.M. Brown
457 R. Scarborough
458 John & Margaret
    Turner
459 Mrs B. Nichols

460 Mrs B. Denman
461 J.M. Adams
462 Mrs J. Clark
463 Mrs Eileen Stacey
464 H.N. Howe
465 David A. Walmsley
466 Richard B. Dodson
467 Rev J. Ambrose Wall
468 Anthony Peers
    Fothergill
469 Harry & Erica Taylor
470 A.N. Cass
471 Rev Bernard W.
    Blanchard
472 D. Lockwood
473 D.J. Bartholomew
474 Devena Mary Wright
475 George & Margaret
    Moulton
476 Mrs M. Harrison
477 Miss G.H. Wilkinson
478 K.A. Whitaker
479 John Wilson
480 Barbara Odling
481 G.H. Bradley
482 Mr & Mrs R.G. Agar
483 Arnold Pacey
484 Rev Kenneth R. Brown
    MA
485 Mrs Sylvia Cook
486 Mrs M. Simpson
487 Mrs Mary Ibbetson
488 Michael Hill
489 Rev Philip J. Wren
490 Anthony R. Walton
491 Joan Borrill
492 Christopher J. Renshaw
493 Mrs Roselle Lamle
494 Mr & Mrs B.G.
    Beardsell
495 Mr & Mrs A. Hibbs
496 Mr & Mrs J. Naylor
497 K.D. Johnson
498 Methodist Archives
499 Wesley Historical
    Society
500 Sarah & Peter
    Thornton
501 F.T. Baker OBE MA
    FSA FMA
502 Mrs Margaret Driver
503 R.W. Dales
504
505 M.G. White
506 Lincolnshire
509 Library Service
510 Rev Ronald Cheffings
511 Manfred Lasser
512 M. G. Pearson
Remaining names unlisted

ENDPAPERS — FRONT: Itinerant & Local Preachers' Plan, Spilsby
Circuit, 1814; BACK: Grimsby Primitive Methodist Plan, 1820.

GRIMSBY BRANCH of the NOTTINGHAM CIRCUIT.

The Lord's Day Plan of the Preachers called Primitive Methodists,

KNOWN ALSO by the NAME of RANTERS.

"Pray ye therefore the Lord of the Harvest that he will send forth labourers into his Harvest." Matt. ix. 38.

1820. PLACES AND TIMES OF PREACHING.	OCTOBER. 1	8	15	22	29	NOVEM. 5	12	19	26	DECEM. 3	10	17	24
Grimsby 2 and 6.	3	1	1	2	2	3c	3	1	1T	2	2	3	3
Louth 10 and 6. Legburn 2.	1		2		3	1c		2			3		1
Legburn 10. Louth 2 and 6.		2		3		1		2		2T		1	
Kennington 2. Limber 6.		3		1		2c		3		1		2	
Binbrook 2	10		3		19		2c		13		1		18
Wales by 2.	2			1c				3				2
Tealby 6.	2		3		1c		2		3		1		2
Barnoldby 2. Waltham 6.	18	10		17		8		6		9		19
Waltham 2.		9		11		6		12		16		7
Holton 2.	7		6		8		9		18		17		12
Thoresby 2. Tetney 6.	11		9		13		19		16		18		17
Fulstow 10. Covenham 2.		7		10		13		9		12		17
Laceby 2.		6		12		11		14		15		9
Swallow 10. Irby 2.	16	17		6		15		11		20		10
Immingham 10. Stallingbro' 2.	17	15		14		12		9		11		15
Ludford 6.	10	16		20		18		10		16		20

PREACHERS' NAMES.

1.—T. King.
2.—G. Herod.
3.—T. Blaides.
4.—A. Carr, ⎫
5.—H. Parrott, ⎪ Local Preachers.
6.—J. Stovin, ⎬
7.—E. Brown, ⎪
8.—J. Scholey, ⎭

⎰ ON TRIAL. ⎱
9.—W. Holt.
10 --B. Hemstock.
11.—G. Swales.

EXHORTERS.
12.—J. Faulding.
13.—G. Norriss.
14.—W. Medcalf.
15.—G. Medcalf.
16.—P. Otterwell.
17.—J. H. 18.—R. W.
19.—F. H. 20.—* *

Lovefeasts.

Holton, October 15
Laceby, November 5
Fulstow, November 5
Barnoldby, November 26
Kennington, December...... 3
Binbrook, December........10
Legburn, December 10
Grimsby, December........17

Quarterly Meeting

At Grimsby, 18th December, to commence at ten o'Clock in the Forenoon. Preachers' Meeting in the Afternoon. Watch Night to begin at 7 o'Clock.

N. B. Every Preacher is affectionately requested to attend his appointments, or provide an approved Substitute.

Sacraments.

Louth, October 1
Grimsby, October ... 8

c —Collection.
T—Tickets.

Squire, Printer, Grimsby.